Praise for

THOMAS JEFFERSON
P·R·E·S·I·D·E·N·T
&
PHILOSOPHER

"Comprehensive and engaging." —*Scholastic Instructor*

"Readers will be rewarded with a coherent, well-supported explanation of a complex man." —*School Library Journal*

"There is a surprising paucity of books about Jefferson at this level . . . and this handsome, well-written, and engaging volume fills that literary gap." —*The Horn Book*

"Offers thoughtful discussions of multifaceted topics. . . . A solid resource for young people intrigued by Jefferson." —*Booklist*

"Wonderfully written and crafted. . . . Entertaining for both kids and adults alike." —*KidsReads.com*

"Interesting, well-written, and provides a detailed and well-documented look at one of our nation's most fascinating historical figures." —*Library Media Connection*

Praise for

THOMAS JEFFERSON: THE ART OF POWER

"Probably the best single-volume biography of Jefferson ever written." —Gordon S. Wood

"Surely there is not a significant detail out there, in any pertinent archive, that [Meacham] has missed."
—*The Washington Post*

"[Meacham] captures who Jefferson was, not just as a statesman but as a man. . . . By the end of the book . . . the reader is likely to feel as if he is losing a dear friend. . . . [An] absorbing tale." —*The Christian Science Monitor*

"A true triumph. In addition to being a brilliant biography, this book is a guide to the use of power. . . . Fascinating."
—Walter Isaacson

"Nuanced and persuasive." —*The New York Times*

"Fascinating and insightful. . . . Many books have been written about Jefferson's life, but few have created such a vivid portrait." —*The Associated Press*

"An excellent biography—expansive, smart and accessible."
—*The Dallas Morning News*

THOMAS JEFFERSON
PRESIDENT
& PHILOSOPHER

in the Course of human events it becomes necessary for one people to dissolve the political bands which have conn
te and equal station to which the Laws of Nature and of Nature's God entitle them, a decent respect to the opin
the separation. —————— We hold these truths to be self-evident, that all men are created equal; tha
these are Life, Liberty and the pursuit of Happiness.— That to secure these rights, Governments are institute
whenever any Form of Government becomes destructive of these ends, it is the Right of the People to alter or to
inciples and organizing its powers in such form, as to them shall seem most likely to effect their Safety and
hould not be changed for light and transient causes; and accordingly all experience hath shewn, that mank
abolishing the forms to which they are accustomed. But when a long train of abuses and usurpations, pur
Despotism, it is their right, it is their duty, to throw off such Government, and to provide new Guards for the
nd such is now the necessity which constrains them to alter their former Systems of Government. The hist
usurpations, all having in direct object the establishment of an absolute Tyranny over these States. To prove
Assent to Laws, the most wholesome and necessary for the public good. —————— He has forbidden his G
their operation till his Assent should be obtained; and when so suspended, he has utterly neglected to attend to t
districts of people, unless those people would relinquish the right of Representation in the Legislature, a right in
legislative bodies at places unusual, uncomfortable, and distant from the depository of their public Records, for
has dissolved Representative Houses repeatedly, for opposing with manly firmness his invasions on the rights of the
ers to be elected; whereby the Legislative powers, incapable of Annihilation, have returned to the People at large
of invasion from without, and convulsions within. —————— He has endeavoured to prevent the population of
fusing to pass others to encourage their migrations hither, and raising the conditions of new Appropriations of La
to Laws for establishing Judiciary powers. —————— He has made Judges dependent on his Will alone, for the
as erected a multitude of New Offices, and sent hither swarms of Officers to harrass our people, and eat out their
the Consent of our legislatures. —————— He has affected to render the Military independent of and superior to the Ci
to our constitution, and unacknowledged by our laws; giving his Assent to their Acts of pretended Legislation
one, by a mock Trial, from punishment for any Murders which they should commit on the Inhabitants of
imposing Taxes on us without our Consent: —— For depriving us in many cases, of the benefits of Trial by
abolishing the free System of English Laws in a neighbouring Province, establishing therein an Arbitrary gov
thument for introducing the same absolute rule into these Colonies: —— For taking away our Charters, ab
nments: —— For suspending our own Legislatures, and declaring themselves invested with power to legis
ing us out of his Protection and waging War against us. —————— He has plundered our seas, ravaged our coasts
ting large Armies of foreign Mercenaries to compleat the works of death, desolation and tyranny, already begun wit
totally unworthy the Head of a civilized nation. —————— He has constrained our fellow Citizens taken Captive
nds and Brethren, or to fall themselves by their Hands. —————— He has excited domestic insurrections amongst us
avages, whose known rule of warfare, is an undistinguished destruction of all ages, sexes and conditions. In
rms. Our repeated Petitions have been answered only by repeated injury. A Prince, whose character is thus marked by
we been wanting in attentions to our British brethren. We have warned them from time to time of attempts by
m of the circumstances of our emigration and settlement here. We have appealed to their native justice and magna
these usurpations, which, would inevitably interrupt our connections and correspondence. They too have bee
in the necessity, which denounces our Separation, and hold them, as we hold the rest of mankind, Enemies in
es of the united States of America, in General Congress, Assembled, appealing to the Supreme Judge
good People of these Colonies, solemnly publish and declare, That these United Colonies are, and of Right
nce to the British Crown, and that all political connection between them and the State of Great Britain, is an
y have full Power to levy War, conclude Peace, contract Alliances, establish Commerce, and to do all other Acts a

THOMAS JEFFERSON

P·R·E·S·I·D·E·N·T
& PHILOSOPHER

JON MEACHAM

Adapted by SARAH L. THOMSON

A YEARLING BOOK

To Mary, Maggie, and Sam

For his expert assistance, grateful acknowledgment to Herbert Sloan, professor of history at Barnard College and member of the advisory board of the Robert H. Smith International Center for Jefferson Studies

Visit us on the Web! randomhousekids.com

Educators and librarians, for a variety of teaching tools, visit us at RHTeachersLibrarians.com

The Library of Congress has cataloged the hardcover edition of this work as follows:
Meacham, Jon.
Thomas Jefferson : president and philosopher / Jon Meacham.
pages cm.
Summary: "In this special illustrated edition of the #1 New York Times bestselling Thomas Jefferson: The Art of Power by Pulitzer Prize–winning author Jon Meacham, young readers will learn about the life and political philosophy of one of our Founding Fathers." —Provided by publisher.
ISBN 978-0-385-38749-1 (trade) — ISBN 978-0-385-38750-7 (lib. bdg.) — ISBN 978-0-385-38751-4 (ebook)
1. Jefferson, Thomas, 1743–1826—Juvenile literature. 2. Presidents—United States—Biography—Juvenile literature. 3. United States—Politics and government—1783–1809—Juvenile literature. I. Title.
E332.M478 2014 973.4'6092—dc23 [B] 2013046973

ISBN 978-0-385-38752-1 (pbk.)

Printed in the United States of America
10 9 8 7 6 5 4 3 2 1
First Yearling Edition 2016

Dear Reader:

Thomas Jefferson once wrote a young relative: "An honest heart being the first blessing, a knowing head is the second." Part of the power of Jefferson to fascinate us all these years distant is rooted in the equal attention this most versatile of our Founders paid to both heart and head, to soul and mind, to philosophy and politics. As those who read the following pages will find, Jefferson is one of the most complicated and riveting human beings who ever drew breath, and few people have left a larger and more enduring mark on the way we live now.

History can sometimes seem dry and distant. It shouldn't, because history, told well and taught properly, is the very human story of flawed people who, at their best, struggled amid the all-too-familiar difficulties of life to leave the world at least a slightly better place than they found it.

This edition of the book is heavily illustrated and includes new features to make the Jefferson saga—and the American saga—more accessible to younger readers. There is a family tree, a timeline of events, and special sections about Jefferson's "inventions" and writings.

When I was a child growing up in Chattanooga, Tennessee, I was already intrigued by history. My family lived on Missionary Ridge, the Civil War battlefield, and we could still find minié balls—bullets—that had been fired there between Confederate and Union forces. For me, then, history was quite real, a tactile matter, and I read book after book on the American story, from Howard Fast's *April Morning* to Esther Forbes's *Johnny Tremain*. Before long, I was consuming biographies of great leaders, including George Washington, Andrew Jackson, Abraham Lincoln, Winston Churchill—and, yes, Thomas Jefferson.

I hope young readers will find this adaptation of my Jefferson biography to be an engaging tale about a man who did extraordinary things but was far from superhuman. I hope they come away understanding a bit more about how America came to be—and what we can still become. I hope they see at least a bit of themselves in Jefferson—in his eclectic interests, his fascination with macaroni and with ice cream, with farming and with art, with inventions and with friendships.

"The qualifications for self-government in society are not innate," Jefferson once wrote. "They are the result of habit and long training." I mostly hope that this book will be just the beginning of a long, exciting, and diverting training in citizenship and historical passion for those who encounter Jefferson here for the first time. An early habit for history is a good thing—and something of which Thomas Jefferson himself would heartily approve.

Jon Meacham

CONTENTS

The Art of Power

Thomas Jefferson believed in America and in Americans. He was a farmer, lawyer, lawmaker, governor, diplomat, secretary of state, vice president, and president. The nation, he said in his first speech as president, was "the world's best hope." He thought Americans themselves were able to do nearly anything they put their minds to. "Whatever they can, they will," Jefferson said of his countrymen.

He had a vision for his country that drove him all his life: the survival and success of government by the people in the United States of America. He believed that the will of the majority should rule, that ordinary Americans would be the soul of the nation and the hope of the country. And that their freedom was in their own hands.

The presentation of the draft of the Declaration of Independence in 1776, as envisioned by artist John Trumbull.

This portrait of Thomas Jefferson was painted during his service in the Continental Congress in 1776.

To make his vision come true, Jefferson needed power. Power means bending the world to one's will. This is the kind of power that Jefferson sought and found.

Jefferson knew how to come up with ideas, and he knew how to convince others to believe in his dreams. He was practical. To shape his dreams into reality, he made deals and compromises. He tried new and unexpected strategies. At any moment, he was willing to do whatever needed to be done. Jefferson was a philosopher who could think; he was also a politician who could plot and plan to put his thoughts into action.

This is the art of power.

❧ ☙

Thomas Jefferson loved his wife, his books, his farms, good wine, architecture, horseback riding, history, France, the Commonwealth of Virginia, spending money, and the very latest in ideas. A philosopher and a scientist, a naturalist and a historian, Jefferson was always looking forward, always eager to learn something new. He adored detail, noting the temperature each day and carrying a tiny notebook in his pocket to write down all the money he spent.

He drove his horses hard and fast and believed that the sun was the best doctor for any illness. He loved walking, drank perhaps three glasses of wine a day, and did not smoke. When he received gifts of cigars, he would pass them along to his friends.

Jefferson was never tired of creating and learning. He designed dumbwaiters and hidden devices to open doors at his Virginia plantation, Monticello. He was fascinated by archaeology (the study of the physical remains of the past), paleontology (the study of fossils and ancient life-forms), astronomy (the study of the stars), botany (the study of plants), and meteorology (the study of Earth's atmosphere). He loved music and gardening and buying or creating beautiful things; he drew the plans for his mansion himself.

Jefferson liked pasta, wrote down a French recipe for ice cream, and enjoyed the search for a perfect dressing for his salads. He kept shepherd dogs (two favorites were named Bergere and Grizzle). He knew Latin, Greek, French, Italian, and Spanish.

A guest at a country inn was said to have once struck up a conversation with a "plainly-dressed" man he did not recognize. The two covered subject after subject, and the guest was amazed by how much the other man knew. When they talked about law, he decided his companion must be a lawyer. When they discussed medicine, he felt sure he was talking to a doctor.

This is a notebook Jefferson used to record daily observations and expenditures.

When the topic was religion, he thought he must be speaking to a minister.

Later on, the guest asked the landlord of the inn whom, exactly, he had been speaking with. The reply was brief: "Oh, I thought you knew the Squire."

"The Squire" was Thomas Jefferson.

Jefferson drew the plans for his mansion, Monticello, himself. This is an early rough sketch from 1770. *Monticello* is Italian for "little mountain."

CHAPTER ONE

A Fortunate Son

It is the strong in body who are both the strong and free in mind.
—PETER JEFFERSON, FATHER OF THOMAS JEFFERSON

Thomas Jefferson's father, Peter, was the kind of man people noticed. He was an excellent rider and hunter, well off and well liked, known for his feats of strength. He owned large plots of land and many slaves. Along the Rivanna River in Virginia, he built a plantation called Shadwell.

Peter Jefferson's family had immigrated to Virginia from England in 1612, and they had done well in the New World.

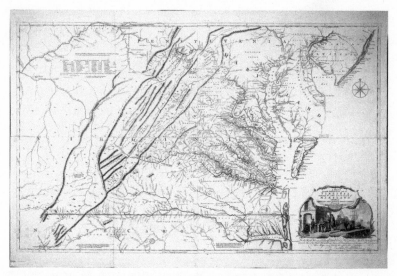

A map of Virginia and Maryland, drawn in 1752 by Joshua Fry and Peter Jefferson, Thomas Jefferson's father.

Peter, born in 1708, continued that tradition. The years between 1700 and 1750 were a thrilling time to be young, white, male, wealthy, and Virginian. Money was to be made, tobacco to be planted and sold, land and slaves to be bought. As a planter and as a surveyor, whose job was to take accurate measurements of land to be used in making maps, Peter Jefferson thrived in Virginia. His oldest son, Thomas, born on April 13, 1743, understood that his father was a man other men admired.

Thomas remembered that his father, by himself, pulled down a wooden shed three slaves had not been able to destroy. It was said that Peter Jefferson had once set upright two huge hogsheads of tobacco, wooden barrels or casks that weighed about a thousand pounds each. On an expedition to settle the boundary between Virginia and North Carolina, Peter and his companions fought off "the attacks of wild beasts during the day, and at night found but a broken rest, sleeping . . . in trees."

Thomas Jefferson grew up with an image of a father who was powerful, who could do things other men could not. The boy admired his father's strength and spent a lifetime telling tales of the older man's daring.

To be like his father, Thomas was taught that he had to be strong. At age ten, the boy was sent into the woods alone with a gun. His job was to come home with proof that he could survive by himself in the wild.

The test did not begin well. He killed nothing. The woods were forbidding. Everything around the boy—the trees and the thickets and the rocks and the river—was frightening and frustrating.

He refused to give up or give in, pushing on until his luck finally changed. The family story went that young Thomas at last found a wild turkey caught in a pen. He used one of the cords that held up his stockings to tie the turkey to a tree, shot it, "and carried it home in triumph."

Taking after his father, Jefferson had an interest in surveying land. This instrument, known as a theodolite, was used by Jefferson to create maps of his Monticello estate.

When he ran into problems, young Thomas was resource-ful. If a first plan failed, he made another plan on the spot. And when he finally reached his goal, he enjoyed his success.

＊ ＊

Peter Jefferson married very well, taking a bride from Virginia's leading family. Jane Randolph, Thomas Jefferson's mother, was the daughter of a planter and sea captain, proud of her British heritage. Their eight children, including Thomas, grew up to live privileged lives. One traveler in Virginia noticed that "the youth of these more indulgent settlements . . . are pampered much more in softness and ease than their neighbors northward."

Wealthy families in Virginia taught their children music and dancing. Thomas sang and played the violin with his older sister Jane. She was his favorite sibling, his "constant companion when home," and music was one of the things they loved to share. "Many a winter evening, round the family fireside, and many a soft summer twilight, on the wooded banks of the Rivanna, heard their voices, accompanied by the notes of his violin."

There were books in Peter Jefferson's study, and young Thomas devoured them—he read Shakespeare, *The History of England* by Paul de Rapin-Thoyras, *Voyage Round the World* by George Anson, *America* by John Ogilvy. Later, a grandson remembered Thomas Jefferson saying that "from the time

One of the books that Thomas Jefferson read as a young boy was *Voyage Round the World* by George Anson. This illustration of Cape Virgin Mary is included in a 1748 edition of *Voyage*.

when, as a boy, he had turned off wearied from play and first found pleasure in a book, he had never sat down in idleness."

As Thomas Jefferson grew, his parents, his teachers, and all the adults he looked up to taught him that a gentleman ought to serve his family, his country, and his king. An eldest son in the Virginia of that time grew up expecting to lead—and to be followed. He was born for command. He never knew anything else.

Jefferson believed that his earliest memory was of being handed up to a slave on horseback and carried, carefully, on a pillow for a long journey. He was two or three at the time. The family was traveling to a plantation called Tuckahoe. The plantation's owner, a cousin of Jane Randolph Jefferson, had just died. Peter Jefferson was keeping a promise he had made to take care of Tuckahoe and of its owner's three young children. His family would stay there for seven years, until Thomas was nine or ten.

Perhaps it was at Tuckahoe that Thomas, growing up in a large combined family and in someone else's house, learned the benefits of getting along with everyone. He did not care for open disagreement and tried to stay out of conflict at almost any cost. "It is a charming thing to be loved by everybody," the adult Jefferson once told one of his grandsons. "And the way to obtain it is, never to quarrel or be angry with anybody."

It was also at Tuckahoe that Thomas began to understand what it meant to grow up in slave-owning Virginia. Years later, he described how the children of slaveholders learned injustice and inequality simply from watching and imitating their parents. "The parent storms, the child looks on . . . [and] puts on the same airs in the circle of smaller slaves," Jefferson remembered. A white child in a house of slaves is "thus nursed, educated, and daily exercised in tyranny."

When Thomas was nine, he was sent away from home to study French and classics, the language and literature of ancient Greek and Rome. His teacher was the Reverend William Douglas, who lived near Tuckahoe. For five years, Thomas lived with Douglas, coming home to his family in the summers.

In 1752, the Jeffersons moved back to their own plantation, Shadwell. Five years later, Peter Jefferson died. The father was forty-nine, and Thomas was fourteen. Immediately the boy had to take on the role of the man of the house. "At 14 years of age the whole care and direction of myself was thrown on my self entirely, without a relative or friend qualified to guide me," he remembered.

There would be no more evenings spent in his father's first-floor study, looking over maps, listening to tales of brave expeditions, tinkering with the tools of surveying, discussing Shakespeare. Those hours with his father were to live only in memory.

Jefferson was born at Shadwell, his family's plantation in Virginia. This marker on U.S. Route 250 notes its location.

This photograph shows archaeologists excavating the site of Jefferson's childhood home at Shadwell.

Shadwell would be run by Thomas's mother, Jane Randolph Jefferson. Fond of books and visitors and lovely things—from fancy silverware and china to elegant furniture and clothing—Jane handled matters as she saw fit. Her oldest child, Jane, was seventeen; her youngest were two-year-old twins. A widow, Jane raised her children and managed her plantation, which had at least 2,750 acres and sixty-six slaves.

"She was an agreeable, intelligent woman, as well educated as the other Virginia ladies of the day . . . and . . . she was a notable housekeeper," wrote one of Jane's great-granddaughters. Jane was also "amiable and affectionate" and had "a lively, cheerful temper" and "a great fund of humor." She was "fond of writing, particularly letters," and she wrote well.

Thomas spent his time at home with his mother or in the home of a second teacher, the Reverend James Maury. He recalled those years warmly, both for the time he spent studying and for the friendships he made. Dabney Carr, a fellow student, became the closest friend of Thomas's youth.

The same age as Thomas, Dabney shared his love for studying, books, and the landscape of Virginia. When they were at the Shadwell plantation, they took their books and climbed through the woods of the mountain that Jefferson later named Monticello, talking and thinking together, until they reached the summit and settled down for a rest under an oak tree. To Jefferson, Dabney Carr was the best of friends. The two young men made a solemn promise— if either of them died, the other would bury his friend's body beneath the oak tree that they both loved.

Jefferson's teacher, Maury, thought that the study of Latin and Greek was necessary for men who would grow up to take jobs or duties "to which the privilege of birth, the voice of their country, or the choice of their prince may call them." In other words, he believed that boys like Thomas Jefferson were born to lead and rule and would need education to help them do so wisely.

Jefferson himself thought there was nothing more important than learning. If he had to choose, he once said, he would take the education his father had arranged for him over the plantation and property his father had left him.

Thomas Jefferson was nearly seventeen when he arrived for the holidays at Chatsworth, a plantation belonging to his mother's cousin. During the visit, the older cousin gave the younger one some advice: to enroll at the College of William and Mary, in nearby Williamsburg. "By going to the College," Jefferson wrote, "I can pursue my studies in the Greek and Latin . . . and likewise learn something of the mathematics."

The college required students who wished to study there to "have made due progress in their Latin and Greek. . . . And let no blockhead or lazy fellow in his studies be elected."

Jefferson was not lazy or a blockhead. And so he left home in 1760, bound for Williamsburg. The city was the capital of Virginia, and it was home to government offices, theaters, taverns—and to a circle of men who would change Jefferson's life forever.

This engraving depicts Wren Hall at the College of William and Mary.

WILLIAM & MARY COLLEGE, WILLIAMSBURG, VA.

CHAPTER TWO

What Fixed the Destinies of My Life

The best news I can tell you is that Williamsburg begins to brighten up and look very clever.
—PEYTON RANDOLPH, COUSIN OF THOMAS JEFFERSON

Williamsburg, the capital of the British colony of Virginia, suited Jefferson perfectly. The latest books were read there. Powerful men and charming women lived there. Jefferson gambled on horses, hunted foxes, gossiped, courted, and danced. And he was introduced to the glamour and drama of politics.

To Jefferson, this was the great world. He studied at William and Mary from age seventeen to nineteen. He was then in and out of the city for five more years as he studied law. The ideas and political lessons he learned in Williamsburg influenced him the rest of his life.

The College Yard at William and Mary, circa 1733.

It was said that Jefferson studied fifteen hours a day, waking up at dawn and reading until two o'clock in the morning. Time spent at study, he believed, was never wasted. "Knowledge," he once wrote, "indeed is a desirable, a lovely possession."

At the college, Jefferson most admired his teacher of science and mathematics. "It was my great good fortune and what probably fixed the destinies of my life, that Dr. William Small of Scotland, was then professor of mathematics," Jefferson wrote later. Small had "a happy talent of communication," along with "correct and gentlemanly manners."

Portrait of Dr. William Small, professor at William and Mary, who taught Jefferson about the writers, scientists, and thinkers of the Enlightenment.

In addition to science and mathematics, Small also taught ethics—ways of thinking about moral choices in order to live a good and useful life. From Small, Jefferson learned a remarkable way of thinking about the world: that human beings should rely on reason, not on priests, kings, or tradition, in deciding what to do about their own affairs.

Jefferson was fascinated by this new idea. Later, he paid Small the highest of compliments, saying that he was "to me . . . a father."

After his college years were over, Jefferson moved on to study law with George Wythe, one of Virginia's greatest lawyers. Hawk-nosed and "of the middle size," Wythe was wise and full of curiosity. "Mr. Wythe continued to be my faithful and beloved mentor in youth, and my most affectionate friend through life," Jefferson recalled.

Wythe was a teacher in elegance as well as law. He had expensive taste, sending to London for satin cloaks for his wife, velvet breeches and silk stockings for himself, and for them both "an elegant set of table and tea china, with bowls of the same of different sizes, decanters and drinking glasses, a handsome service of glass for a dessert, four middle-sized and six lesser dishes and . . . a handsome well-built chariot." The Wythes also loved to entertain. "Mrs. Wythe puts 1/10 very rich Malmsey to a dry Madeira and makes a fine wine," Jefferson once noted with appreciation.

Portrait of George Wythe, who was Jefferson's law teacher, colleague, and friend. The two men shared a love of learning, the law, and fine things.

George Wythe and William Small were not Jefferson's only teachers. Thomas Jefferson regarded meeting every new person as a chance to learn something. He was always asking questions, about "the construction of a wheel or the anatomy of an extinct species of animals." After the conversation, he'd hurry home to make notes of what he had heard. He was soon known as a "walking encyclopedia."

Jefferson may have spent a great deal of his time studying and learning, but it was not all that he did. He enjoyed company and was a happy member of the Flat Hat Club at William and Mary. This secret society had, as Jefferson put it, "no useful object" or goal.

Jefferson also believed in the value of riding and walking, holding that a strong, healthy body creates a strong mind. While in Williamsburg, he exercised by running to a particular stone a mile from town; home at Shadwell, he rowed a small canoe of his own design across the Rivanna River and climbed the mountain he was later to call Monticello. "Not less than two hours a day should be devoted to exercise, and the weather should be little regarded," he once said. "A person not sick will not be injured by getting wet. It is but taking a cold bath, which never gives a cold to any one." For Jefferson, laziness was a sin.

The young Jefferson could play as hard as he worked. "I was often thrown into the society of horse racers, and card players, fox hunters," he remembered later. "Many a time have I asked myself . . . Well, which of these kinds of reputation should I prefer? That of a horse jockey? A fox hunter? An orator [a fine public speaker]? Or the honest advocate of my country's rights?"

The truth was that he could be all these things. The way Jefferson spent his Williamsburg years suggests that he knew how to seek knowledge and pleasure at the same time.

He found both at the Governor's Palace. Francis Fauquier was the royal governor of Virginia, appointed by the king of England. About the age of Thomas Jefferson's father, Fauquier loved science, fine food, good music, and spirited card playing. The governor often invited Jefferson's teachers William Small and George Wythe to his table. Jefferson was included. There was dinner, conversation, and music. Jefferson brought his violin and was sometimes asked to perform.

Many close to Jefferson thought that he owed his polished manners and ease in society to those years spent socializing with the governor of Virginia and his guests. For the rest of his life, Jefferson tried to find, again and again, the good food, conversation, and companionship of those long Williamsburg nights. At his round dining table in Monticello, in the salons of Paris, in boardinghouses and taverns in Philadelphia and New York, and

Francis Fauquier was the royal governor of Virginia when Jefferson was a student. He invited Jefferson to attend intimate dinners and encouraged him to continue playing the violin.

The Governor's Palace in Williamsburg, Virginia, took sixteen years to build and was finally completed in 1722.

finally at the President's House in Washington, D.C., Jefferson loved talk of the latest in science and the arts. He adored conversation with the men, and the beautiful women, who made the world run on both sides of the Atlantic.

One of those men who made the world run was his cousin Peyton Randolph, a lawyer and politician. Randolph was friendly, outgoing, and impressive. One observer called him "large in size, though not out of proportion. . . . [He] commands respect and esteem."

Small, Wythe, Fauquier, and Randolph became the standard by which Jefferson judged everyone else. "Under

Portrait of Peyton Randolph, known as "The Speaker." He served as Speaker of the House of Burgesses and various Virginia assemblies in the early Revolutionary era.

16

temptations and difficulties," Jefferson later told a grandson, "I would ask myself—what would Dr. Small, Mr. Wythe, Peyton Randolph, do in this situation?" *What would these men approve of? Jefferson would ask. What would they want me to do?*

Always busy with family, friends, and callers, Jefferson enjoyed being at the center of everything, no matter what the everything was. His own identity, he believed, was a part of society, and he never wanted to be away from that society for long. "I am convinced that our own happiness requires that we should continue to mix with the world, and to keep pace with it as it goes," he once wrote to one of his daughters. Company with those we respect and love, he said, "informs the mind, sweetens the temper, cheers our spirits, and promotes health."

Mixing with the world sometimes meant heartbreak. For a time in the early 1760s, Jefferson was passionately in love with a young woman named Rebecca Lewis Burwell, the sister of a classmate. But little about the courtship went well. Even rats and rain seemed to conspire against him. On Christmas Eve in 1762, Jefferson (on a visit to his brother-in-law's) went to bed, leaving his garters, pocketbook, and watch in his room. Inside the watch was a paper drawing of Rebecca.

Awakening on Christmas morning, Jefferson discovered that rats had gotten into his room and gnawed on his pocketbook and garters. Worse, rain had leaked through the roof, soaking his watch and destroying Rebecca's picture. To the lovesick Jefferson, both events seemed like terrible omens.

"Is there any such thing as happiness in this world?" he wondered, and he answered himself: "No." About a month later, back home at Shadwell, he was still gloomy. "All things here appear to me to trudge on in one and the same round: we rise in the morning that we may eat breakfast, dinner, and supper and go to bed again that we may get up the next morning and do the same: so that you never saw two peas more alike than our yesterdays and to-day," he complained to a school friend.

His feelings for Rebecca grew stronger as the year went on. In October 1763, Jefferson decided to ask her to marry him.

There was a dance that evening in the Raleigh Tavern in Williamsburg, with its brightly lit banqueting hall. In this elegant setting, Jefferson believed that the time was right. "I was prepared to say a great deal," he remembered. "I had dressed up in my own mind such thoughts as occurred to me, in as moving language as I knew how." He was dancing with the woman he loved among people he liked. Everything appeared set.

He tried to speak, and it all fell apart. He could say only "a few broken sentences." Later, he made another attempt, a conversation where, he said, he "opened my mind more freely and more fully." But he still couldn't speak directly of what he wanted. "I asked no question which would admit of a categorical answer," he remembered, "but assured [her] that such questions would one day be asked." In fact, Jefferson asked no more questions of Rebecca. He never had another private conversation with her. By spring, she was engaged to marry someone else.

After losing Rebecca, Jefferson experienced a painful, long-lasting headache; over time, this would become a familiar response to stress and anxiety. He needed to get his mind off his lost love. Fortunately for him, he was a man of wide interests, and his teachers and mentors were encouraging those interests as his lovesickness faded.

headaches

Established in 1717, the Raleigh Tavern hosted festive balls where colonial Virginians would spend evenings dancing.

CHAPTER THREE

Roots of Revolution

Our minds were circumscribed within narrow limits by an habitual belief that it was our duty to be subordinate to the mother country.
—THOMAS JEFFERSON

To follow Thomas Jefferson in the 1760s and early 1770s is to see how the American Revolution took shape, and why. Vital questions were being debated everywhere in America when Jefferson was a young adult. What did liberty mean? How could, and how should, people have a voice in their own government?

The king of England held power over the American colonies. The British controlled trade and transportation. They set taxes. Royal governors of the colonies could call assemblies with elected representatives. But the governors could veto any laws such assemblies made. They could also dissolve the assemblies at any time they chose, sending the representatives home. The British subjects living in the colonies of North America could not elect any representatives to the British Parliament, where the laws of England were made.

Americans who knew their British history (and, since they were British, most of them did) thought of that history as a long struggle to save the freedoms of individual men and women from the overreaching control of kings, queens, and nobles. Thomas Jefferson had inherited a book from his father: Paul de Rapin-Thoyras's *History of England*. The author's view of England's past showed a battle between a powerful monarchy and a government that better represented the wishes of the people.

Jefferson took this division seriously. Later, he would argue that all societies are likely to be divided into those who want a powerful king and those who want the people to be the final power.

Americans of Jefferson's time were suspicious of the power of the British Crown. The monarch needed to be balanced by Parliament, with representatives chosen by the people. (Not all the members of the British Parliament were elected,

THE FRENCH AND INDIAN WAR

The French and Indian War was part of a larger struggle between Great Britain and France over who would control the New World. England and France were old rivals, and each wanted to rule a vast empire. They believed that North America was a vital piece of that empire.

British and American troops clashed with French soldiers and their Native American allies until the French were defeated. The signing of the Treaty of Paris formally ended the fighting in 1763. The treaty divided the eastern part of North America between Great Britain and Spain. Great Britain took control of French territory east of the Mississippi River, including Canada. Spain handed over Florida to Great Britain (although it took back this territory after the Revolutionary War) and in return received the Louisiana Territory.

but some were.) Judges who owed loyalty to the law rather than the Crown were also important. Without Parliament and a system of judges to restrain its power, a monarchy could easily become a tyranny, crushing the hard-won rights of individuals. It was something Americans were on the watch for.

By the end of the French and Indian War, American disagreements with England over taxes broke out afresh. England had won the war, wresting control over North America from the French. But now the British government faced a struggle with its own colonies.

About ten thousand British troops remained in the American colonies once the fighting was over. The presence of the soldiers felt like a threat. Were they there to protect the colonists or rule over them? New laws and policies from England seemed designed to keep tighter control on the colonies, over everything from grants of land in the West to the right of British agents to board and search American ships.

The Sugar Act of 1764 set new taxes on the colonies (including one on Madeira wine, a favorite of Thomas Jefferson's). The Stamp Act of 1765 taxed documents and anything made of paper, even newspapers and playing cards. These acts were not just a device to raise money for the British government, although it needed money badly. They were also designed to make it clear that the Crown had the right to tax its American subjects in any way it saw fit.

Thomas Jefferson was there to watch the action in the Virginia House of Burgesses. The members of this assembly,

A group of angry colonists, including merchants and shopkeepers, protest the Stamp Act of 1765.

Jefferson's political education began when he listened to Patrick Henry protest the Stamp Act in 1765.

elected to make laws for the colony, were debating how to respond to the Stamp Act. Jefferson listened, fascinated, as a lawyer named Patrick Henry took the floor, arguing passionately that the Stamp Act was tyranny. When the Speaker of the House told Henry that his words were treason, he backed down. "He was ready to ask pardon, and he would show his loyalty to His Majesty King George III at the expense of the last drop of his blood," Henry promised. But he had spoken out of concern for "his country's dying liberty, which he had at heart."

Patrick Henry did not achieve his aim, which was to have the House of Burgesses send England a resolution opposing the Stamp Act. But a sense of opposition to the monarchy was growing stronger. When Thomas Jefferson's friend Governor Fauquier gave his yearly ball in honor of King George III's birthday, it was not the usual spectacular event. "I went there in expectation of seeing a great deal of company," one of the guests complained, "but was disappointed for there were not above a dozen people. I came away before supper."

As tension between England and her American colonies grew, Thomas Jefferson watched famous speakers like Patrick

Henry change minds and stir emotions, but he knew he had no great talent for public speaking himself. Instead, he taught himself other ways to reach out to people, learning to write with skill and conviction and, importantly, speed.

Jefferson connected with others by offering them what they wanted most: an audience to listen to their own vision and views. Politicians often talk too much and listen too little. Not Jefferson. A grandson remembered how Jefferson always turned the conversation "to subjects most familiar" with his companions. Whatever they wanted to talk about was what he wanted to hear.

When Jefferson was invited to dinner with "a most intelligent and dignified Virginia matron," he always asked how her best dishes were cooked. She knew he was trying to charm her. "I knew this was half to please me," she admitted. But the charm worked. Jefferson showed with her, as with many others, that he knew how to engage people.

❧ ❦

The fall of 1765 should have been a joyful time for Jefferson. In the summer of that year, his sister Martha had married his old friend Dabney Carr. Jefferson was delighted by the marriage. Young and bright and popular, beloved and respected by his teachers in Williamsburg, with the memory of a failed love affair fading, Jefferson thought the world a mostly happy place.

Then, on Tuesday, October 1, 1765, his sister Jane died.

He had loved Jane, and his grief at losing her was terrible. "The loss of such a sister to such a brother was irreparable," a great-granddaughter wrote later. Jefferson composed a Latin epitaph for his beloved sister, calling her Joanna.

> *Ah, Joanna, best of girls.*
> *Ah, torn away from the bloom of vigorous age.*
> *May the earth be light upon you.*
> *Farewell, forever and ever.*

Nearly six months after Jane died, Jefferson began keeping his garden book. In it, he wrote everything he noticed about the life—and death—of his flowers and vegetables. He longed for spring. "Purple hyacinth begins to bloom," he wrote in March. "Narcissus and Puckoon open," he noted on April 6. A week later, the puckoons, or bloodwort, had fallen.

Still mourning Jane, he was torn between staying home and seeing the wider world. As the weeks passed, he planned a journey north, his first outside the borders of Virginia.

Setting out in the spring, Jefferson endured a perilous trip. Twice on the first day, his horse broke away from

A page from Jefferson's garden book, in which he observed the life of his plants.

him, "greatly endanger[ing] the breaking [of] my neck." The second day brought terrible rains, and Jefferson could find no shelter on the road. While crossing a stream, he was nearly swamped by unexpectedly deep water. He was among strangers, too. For the first time in his life, he was seeing "no face known to me before."

He stopped in Annapolis, Maryland, which he found "extremely beautiful," and visited the colonial assembly. A bit snobbishly, he noticed that the Speaker's wig was old and yellowed; he thought that the man had "very little the air of a speaker." But he was fascinated to witness the assembly's joy on hearing the news that the British government had decided to repeal the unpopular Stamp Act.

Although the Parliament in London had abolished the tax, it had also passed a declaration announcing that it possessed the power to tax its colonies "in all cases whatsoever." Hearing this news while traveling in a new state showed Jefferson that the American story, and the American cause, were larger than Williamsburg, and larger than Virginia. The struggle with the British king over taxes involved every American colony and every American.

❧ ❧

In 1767, Jefferson finished his study of the law with George Wythe and became a lawyer. He lived at Shadwell with his mother but traveled often. People who knew him remembered him as a bright, enthusiastic, and curious lawyer, taking whatever cases came his way. (One of those cases involved the theft of a bottle of whiskey and a shirt.)

Jefferson's friends loved him, his clients appreciated him, and his elders admired him. He was the kind of man others thought well of and believed they could trust—unless, as one of his best friends was about to discover, a beautiful young wife was in the picture.

CHAPTER FOUR

Temptations and Trials

You will perceive that I plead guilty to one of their charges,
that when young and single I offered love to a handsome lady.
—THOMAS JEFFERSON

Jefferson was too much in love (or thought he was) to care that the woman he loved was married to someone else. He wanted what he wanted, and he did not give up easily.

Elizabeth Walker was what he wanted. She was the wife of his friend John Walker. The two men had gone to school and college with one another. "We had previously grown up together at a private school and our . . . acquaintance was strengthened at college," John Walker recalled. "We loved (at least I did sincerely) each other."

By 1768, the Walkers and their infant daughter were living at their plantation, Belvoir, only five miles or so from Shadwell. Like Jefferson, Walker was a rising man in Virginia politics. He agreed to travel to New York to join in negotiations with Native American tribes.

Jefferson had just turned twenty-five, and Betsy Walker was two years younger. He visited Belvoir often when John Walker was away and seemed to have fallen in love with his friend's new wife.

Betsy did not return his feelings, but Jefferson did not give up the chase. He wrote her a note, which she tore to pieces. He visited her room, only to be sent away "with indignation and menaces of alarm." Decades later, Jefferson admitted it had been an incorrect thing to do.

❧ ❦

Governor Francis Fauquier died in Williamsburg in March 1768. His burial five days later marked the end of an era for Jefferson and others who had often been guests at the Governor's Palace. It marked a change of government for Virginians, too. Lord Botetourt was appointed the new governor.

At the same time that Jefferson lost Fauquier, his long-time mentor and friend in Williamsburg, he was building a new home for himself two miles from his mother's house at

Shadwell. He named the place Monticello, Italian for "little mountain," and in the summer after Fauquier's death, he reached an agreement to level the top of the little mountain for building.

That winter, Jefferson was elected to the Virginia House of Burgesses, and he first took his seat there in May 1769. He was twenty-six years old and at the start of a career in politics that would last most of his life. He spent most of the next forty-one years in public office.

life / 42 yrs in politics

A photograph of the chamber of the House of Burgesses at the Capitol in Williamsburg, Virginia, where Jefferson began serving in May 1769.

Charles Townshend was the sponsor of four acts passed by the British Parliament and widely resented in the colonies. The acts set taxes on lead, glass, paper, paint, and tea, among other things.

There were serious issues to be debated in the House of Burgesses. The British Parliament had repealed the Stamp Act, but it had since passed a new round of taxes called the Townshend Acts. The colony of Massachusetts led the opposition, and the Massachusetts legislature approved a letter protesting the acts. They called on the other colonies, including Virginia, to do the same. London had ordered the new governor of Virginia, Lord Botetourt, to dissolve the House of Burgesses and send its members home if they did as Massachusetts urged.

The House of Burgesses promptly passed a resolution supporting Massachusetts and opposing the Townshend Acts. Governor Botetourt summoned the lawmakers. "I have heard of your resolutions," he told them. "You have made it my duty to dissolve you; and you are dissolved accordingly."

Jefferson and his colleagues walked to the Raleigh Tavern and tried to decide what to do next. By the next day, they had a plan: they would not buy or import anything at all from Great Britain.

Thomas Jefferson had been a member of the House of Burgesses for ten days.

⇥ ⇤

Jefferson and his fellow Virginians in the House of Burgesses may have been debating their own freedom from England.

But other Virginians had no freedom at all. In 1769, Jefferson placed an advertisement in the *Virginia Gazette* for a runaway slave. He wrote:

> *Run away from the subscriber in* Albermarle, *a Mulatto slave called* Sandy, *about 35 years of age, his stature [height] is rather low, inclining to corpulence [fatness], and his complexion light; he is a shoemaker by trade, in which he uses his left hand principally, can do coarse carpenters work, and is something of a horse jockey. . . . He took with him a white horse . . . he also carried his shoemakers tools, and will probably endeavour [try] to get employment that way. Whoever conveys the said slave to me, in* Albermarle, *shall have 40 s. [shillings] reward, if taken up within the county, 4 l. [pounds] if elsewhere within the colony, and 10 l. if in any other colony, from*
> THOMAS JEFFERSON.

RUN away from the subscriber in *Albemarle*, a Mulatto slave called *Sandy*, about 35 years of age, his stature is rather low, inclining to corpulence, and his complexion light; he is a shoemaker by trade, in which he uses his left hand principally, can do coarse carpenters work, and is something of a horse jockey; he is greatly addicted to drink, and when drunk is insolent and disorderly, in his conversation he swears much, and in his behaviour is artful and knavish. He took with him a white horse, much scarred with traces, of which it is expected he will endeavour to dispose; he also carried his shoemakers tools, and will probably endeavour to get employment that way. Whoever conveys the said slave to me, in *Albemarle*, shall have 40 s. reward, if taken up within the county, 4 l. if elsewhere within the colony, and 10 l. if in any other colony, from
THOMAS JEFFERSON.

Jefferson ran this ad offering a reward for the return of his runaway slave "Sandy" in the *Virginia Gazette* in September 1769.

From about this time until his death, Thomas Jefferson would own more than 600 slaves. He inherited 150 (from his father and father-in-law) and bought roughly 20. Most of the rest were born into slavery on his lands. From 1774 to 1826, Jefferson tended to have about 200 slaves at any one time.

In the beginning of his public career, Jefferson made some attempts to reform slavery. In 1769 in the House of Burgesses, Jefferson recalled, "I made one effort in that body for the permission of the emancipation [freedom] of slaves, which was rejected." The law that Jefferson proposed would not have freed the slaves of Virginia, but it would have made it easier for slaveholders—men like himself—to free their own slaves. Jefferson's bill never became law.

Shortly after this attempt to change the law, Jefferson tried to change one man's life. He was hired as a lawyer by a man who was the grandson of a white woman and a black man, and he argued that his client should live free. "Everyone comes into this world with a right to his own person and using it at his own will," Jefferson insisted. "This is what is called personal liberty, and is given [to] him by the author of nature." Jefferson lost the case.

As a young lawyer and politician eager to succeed, Jefferson must have noticed how soundly he had failed both times he attacked the laws concerning slavery. In the end, he stopped trying to work for change when it came to the enslavement of one race to another.

※ ※

On Thursday, February 1, 1770, Jefferson was with his mother, paying a visit to a neighbor, when word of a disaster reached them. Shadwell had burned.

Jefferson was devastated. His first question to the slave who brought the news was whether his library had been rescued from the flames. The books were all burned, the slave told him, adding, "But, ah! We saved your fiddle!"

Jefferson was always a collector and treasurer of beautiful and valuable things. Now nearly everything he loved was gone. The loss of his books and his legal papers made him frantic, since he was no longer prepared for the law cases he was handling.

He turned to the future, which to him meant Monticello. The summit of his mountain had been cleared for building, and on the southeastern hillside he created an orchard of pear, apple, nectarine, pomegranate, and fig trees.

Jefferson tried to find relief from the pain of losing his home and the hard work of his job in a familiar pastime: flirting. Jefferson, it seemed, was in love.

One of Jefferson's gardens at Monticello. Gardening was one of his favorite pastimes, and the spacious landscape at Monticello offered him plenty of opportunity to cultivate his hobby.

CHAPTER FIVE

A World of Desire and Denial

Harmony in the marriage state is the very first object to be aimed at.
    —THOMAS JEFFERSON

Her name was Martha Wayles Skelton; her friends called her Patty. Her father had been born to a poor family in England but had made a fortune in America as a lawyer, debt collector, slave trader, and planter. Patty's mother had died when she was born, and her father had married two more times, providing the girl with two stepmothers and three half sisters. Patty had been married before she met Jefferson, but her husband and their son had both died, and she had returned as a widow to her father's house.

Beautiful, musical, well read, and intelligent, she was five *← Patty* and a half years younger than Jefferson. "Her complexion was brilliant—her large expressive eyes of the richest shade of hazel—her luxuriant hair of the finest tinge of auburn," one writer described her. She was also remembered as a woman of "good sense and good nature."

Jefferson was determined to make Patty his wife and courted her with attention, music, and conversation. They would sing and play music together, as Jefferson had once done with his sister Jane, and he ordered her a piano for a gift. "Let the case be of fine mahogany," he directed, and he also wanted "plenty of spare strings, and the workmanship of the whole very handsome, and worthy [of] the acceptance of a lady for whom I intend it."

In Patty, Jefferson found a companion who could fully share his life. Their nights were filled with music and wine and talk—talk of everything, including politics. Smart and strong-willed, Patty liked having her way. A granddaughter remembered that Patty's temper might "border on tartness," but her "exceeding affection" for her husband kept her gentle with him.

Jefferson valued harmony and peace too much to indulge in arguments. "Much better . . . if our companion views a thing in a light different from what we do, to leave him in quiet possession of his view," he once told one of his daughters. If the issue was unimportant, he advised, just let it pass. If it *was* important, "wait [for] a softer moment" to talk things over together.

Patty could reassure and calm Jefferson when he was worried or restless. He was sensitive and hated any hint of disapproval or criticism. In his political career, he received his fair share of both. Patty appears to have been one of the few people who could soothe him.

Jefferson married Patty on New Year's Day 1772. He was twenty-eight and she was twenty-three. After their wedding, they stayed at Patty's father's house for one day before making the journey to Monticello. The snow became too deep for their carriage. They switched to horseback and pressed on through the forests and the wind and the snow and the ice and the gathering darkness.

At sunset, they slowly began to climb the mountain. When they arrived at the summit, Monticello was waiting for them.

The house (which Jefferson eventually tore down and rebuilt) had been finished, and it was a grand place. "An elegant building," one visitor called it, and went on to say that it was "built quite recently, in the latest *Italian* style." All his life, Jefferson was on the watch for lovely things to fill his house—a chessboard and pieces, a backgammon table, a telescope, eight Venetian blinds, and a Scotch carpet. And he made sure the library was filled with books.

When the newly married couple arrived that winter evening, however, the house was not as welcoming as Jefferson could have wished. No one was waiting for them. The fires were out and the slaves were elsewhere. "The horrible dreariness of such a house, at the end of such a journey, I have often heard both relate," said one of their daughters.

The Jeffersons discovered part of a bottle of wine, and the rest of the night was "lit up with song, and merriment, and laughter!" They settled in at Monticello. Patty Jefferson was a careful housekeeper, making sure everything ran smoothly. She saw to fresh supplies of meat, eggs, butter, and fruit and supervised the making of beer and soap. She personally directed the work of the kitchen if complicated meals were under way. "Mrs. Jefferson would come out there with a cookery book in her hand and read out of it to Isaac's mother how to make cakes, tarts, and so on," recalled Isaac Granger Jefferson, a slave who left a memoir of life at Monticello.

One guest at Monticello was impressed with Jefferson's library and his designs for the house. He also appreciated the music the couple created. "As all Virginians are fond of music, he is particularly so," the man said of his host. "You will

Jefferson may have used this telescope to observe the landscape of Virginia—and to see British troops arriving in Charlottesville in 1781.

find in his house an elegant harpsichord piano forte [piano] and some violins. The latter he performs well upon himself, the former his lady touches very skillfully."

It was a life of ideas, invention, and music. It was the kind of life that Jefferson had long imagined for himself, the kind that his father had built and his mother had maintained and that he now created for his own family.

On Sunday, May 16, 1773, Jefferson suffered a sharply painful loss. His friend and brother-in-law Dabney Carr died of a fever, leaving Jefferson's sister Martha to raise six children. Jefferson did whatever he could to help his sister's family,

I liked so many things [handwritten annotation]

The kitchen at Monticello as it was in 1809; Patty Jefferson oversaw everything here, from the making of soap to the cooking of meals.

offering shelter and love in the midst of his own sadness. As Dabney and he had agreed long ago, he buried his friend on the mountain of Monticello, where they had walked and talked and read together.

Patty, meanwhile, suffered her own loss. Her father, John Wayles, died that same May. One of the things Patty did following her father's death was to take some of his slaves into her own household, including a woman named Elizabeth Hemings. Elizabeth was the mother of several children, who came with her to Monticello. The children's father was John Wayles. *← Patty's father*

It was common for slave owners to father children with the women they owned, and it was something that was simply not discussed in white society. Patty would not have said openly that the new slaves on her plantation were her half brothers and half sisters. We do not know how she really felt about her father's relationship with Elizabeth Hemings. But we do know that Patty chose to keep the Hemings family together after her father's death. If Patty had not taken Elizabeth and her children to Monticello, they might well have been sold to different owners, never to see each other again.

After this, the Hemings family always had a close relationship with the Jefferson family and with Monticello. Elizabeth's son Robert Hemings, whom Jefferson called Bob, became Jefferson's personal servant. James Hemings would later travel with Jefferson to Paris and work as his chef. John

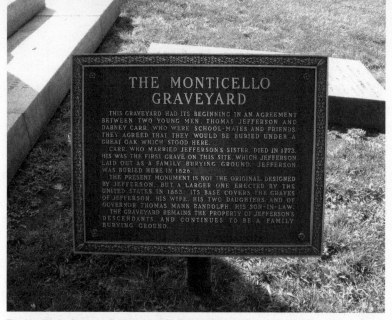

The Monticello Graveyard, where Jefferson buried his brother-in-law Dabney Carr under a large oak tree, which had been a place of fond memories for the two men.

Hemings (often spelled Hemmings) became a skilled carpenter, crafting furniture and a carriage of Jefferson's own design. And Elizabeth's youngest daughter, Sarah, called Sally, would become even more central in Thomas Jefferson's life.

Thomas Jefferson was now a married man, the owner of his own plantation, a slaveholder, a lawyer of note, and a member of the Virginia House of Burgesses. He was about to become a leader of and a voice for a nation in rebellion against the world's greatest empire.

CHAPTER SIX

There Is
No Peace

*Blows must decide whether they are to be subject to this
country or independent.*
—KING GEORGE III, ON THE AMERICAN COLONIES

Thomas Jefferson was not only a husband but a father twice
over. Patty gave birth to a daughter, Martha, called Patsy, in
1772, and to a second daughter, Jane, two years later. But
Jefferson could not spend all his time at Monticello with his
young family. The House of Burgesses was once more allowed
to meet, and he had to be there.

Since Jefferson had taken his seat in the assembly,
a pattern of conflict with England had been growing. The

British Parliament would impose new taxes. Colonists would resist in various ways—writing protests, boycotting British goods. The royal governors of the colonies and the government in Britain became more and more impatient with what they saw as a continent full of stubborn, unreasonable, and ungrateful colonists.

THE BOSTON TEA PARTY

The taxes raised by the Townshend Acts of 1767 had been removed after much protest by the colonists, except for the tax on tea. The British government left that tax in place to prove that it did indeed have the power to tax its colonies. In 1773, the British Parliament passed a new law that allowed only the East India Company to sell its tea in the American colonies. On December 16, 1773, American colonists who had disguised themselves as Mohawk Indians threw 342 chests of tea belonging to the East India Company into Boston Harbor.

This print, titled *The Destruction of Tea at Boston Harbor,* illustrates the events of the Boston Tea Party.

In May 1774, the latest piece of the pattern was announced—the Boston Port Act. This act of Parliament ordered the port of Boston closed until the city paid for the tea thrown into the harbor during the Boston Tea Party.

It was time to take action. Jefferson and his allies in the House thought that what was needed was "a day of general prayer and fasting." This, Jefferson thought, would "call up and alarm the attention" of Virginians to what was happening in Massachusetts. It was effective, Jefferson believed, exactly as he had hoped: "The effect of the day[s] through the whole colony was like a shock of electricity, arousing every man."

In the fall of 1774, Jefferson's participation in the ongoing struggle with Britain was about to get more serious. Representatives from Virginia had been selected to attend the national Continental Congress. (As they began to think of themselves as separate from Great Britain, men like Jefferson began to use the term "continental" to describe the colonies. It meant something that belonged to the North American continent, far from the shores of England.)

At the Congress, elected representatives from all the colonies gathered to discuss how to respond to the actions by the British government. In particular, the colonists objected to what they called the Coercive Acts. Jefferson's job was to compose instructions for the representatives to take with them.

Wow! Tough Laws

THE COERCIVE ACTS

The Coercive Acts, also called the Intolerable Acts, were laws passed by the British Parliament to control the American colonies.

- *The Boston Port Act* closed Boston Harbor until the colonists paid for the tea destroyed during the Boston Tea Party.
- *The Massachusetts Government Act* established a military government in Massachusetts and forbade town meetings without approval.
- *The Administration of Justice Act* allowed British officials who were accused of committing crimes while enforcing British laws to travel to another colony or back to England for trial.
- *The Quartering Act* forced colonists to let British troops stay in their homes.

JOIN, or DIE.

This cartoon was published by Benjamin Franklin in the *Pennsylvania Gazette* in reaction to the Coercive Acts. Franklin wanted the colonies to unite against Britain.

His work, called *A Summary View of the Rights of British America*, was addressed to the king of England. But it was intended to remind all readers that Americans had rights that the Crown could not and should not ignore.

Jefferson was writing, he said, to remind George III "that our ancestors, before their emigration to America, were the free inhabitants of the British dominions in Europe." Those ancestors "had established there that system of laws which has so long been the glory and protection of that country." Jefferson promised loyalty to the king. "It is neither our wish nor our interest to separate from" Great Britain, he said. On the other hand, he insisted on rejecting the British attempts to tax the colonies. Americans should not be taxed "by any power on earth but our own."

A
SUMMARY VIEW
OF THE
RIGHTS
OF
BRITISH AMERICA.
Set forth in some
RESOLUTIONS
INTENDED FOR THE
INSPECTION
OF THE PRESENT
DELEGATES
OF THE
PEOPLE OF VIRGINIA,
NOW IN
CONVENTION.

BY A NATIVE, AND MEMBER OF THE HOUSE OF BURGESSES.
Thomas Jefferson

WILLIAMSBURG: PRINTED:
PHILADELPHIA: Re-Printed by JOHN DUNLAP.

M,DCC,LXXIV.

Jefferson wrote his pamphlet *A Summary View* at Monticello in 1774. It was an early expression of Jefferson's beliefs regarding America's place in the world and was the first time Jefferson was recognized for his superior writing skills.

The colonists hoped that King George III of Britain would help to reconcile Britain and the colonies, but he felt that war was necessary.

He went on: "Let those flatter, who fear; it is not an American art. . . . Let not the name of George the third be a blot in the page of history. . . . The whole art of government consists in the art of being honest. Only aim to do your duty, and mankind will give you credit where you fail."

Jefferson's *Summary View* was published in Williamsburg and spread widely. In August, George Washington paid three shillings and nine pence for several copies of what he called "Mr. Jefferson's Bill of Rights." John Adams called it "a very handsome public paper."

Not everyone agreed with all that Jefferson had said in the *Summary View*. He was pushing for true independence from England. The colonists as a whole were not ready for this. "Tamer sentiments were preferred, and I believe, wisely preferred; the leap I proposed being too long as yet for the mass of our citizens," Jefferson remembered later. Still, Thomas Jefferson was becoming more and more widely known as a man dedicated to the cause of resisting British rule.

At Monticello, the peach trees were blooming. It was early March 1775, and Thomas Jefferson was about to leave for Richmond, Virginia. He was headed for the Virginia Convention, a meeting of revolutionary leaders to be held at St. John's, a wooden Anglican church on top of a hill. A hundred representatives sat in the pews, and eager watchers filled up the church and overflowed into the yard outside.

The work of the convention was to form plans for Virginia in case war broke out with England. They had to make decisions about military preparations, taxes, and trade. Meanwhile, the British government in the colonies was taking a stronger stand against Jefferson and men like him, who were rallying for independence.

Virginia had a new governor, Lord Dunmore, who had forbidden the colonists to buy guns or gunpowder from Britain. Any weapons that arrived in the colony were to be seized. In other colonies, similar conflicts were breaking out. British troops in New England took control of gunpowder and cannons to keep them out of the hands of the colonists. Neither side showed any inclination to back down.

At St. John's, Jefferson listened as Patrick Henry rose to his feet and called on Virginia to prepare for war. "Gentlemen may cry, Peace, Peace—but there is no peace," Henry warned. "The war is actually begun!" In an exhilarating

John Murray, Earl of Dunmore, was the last royal governor of Virginia. He did everything he could to hinder the colonists' efforts for independence, including offering freedom to slaves and servants who fought for the British.

climax, Henry cried out, "I know not what course others may take; but as for me—give me liberty, or give me death!"

To Jefferson, Henry seemed like a magician. His power to move others with the spoken word was incredible, and his speech was "impressive and sublime beyond what can be imagined," he remembered.

Afterward, it fell to a committee that included Jefferson to work out the actual plans for the colony to defend itself. The committee decided:

> that every horseman be provided with a good horse, bridle, saddle with pistols and holsters, a carbine or other short firelock with a bucket, a cutting sword or tomahawk, one pound of gunpowder and four pound of ball at the least, and use the utmost diligence in training and accustoming his horse to stand the discharge of firearms, and in making himself acquainted with the military exercise for cavalry.

In addition to his committee work, Jefferson was elected to the Second Continental Congress. The actions of the first Congress had not had the effect that the colonists hoped for. The British government had not changed any of the laws that they objected to. In fact, the colonists had been forbidden to elect representatives to the Second Continental Congress, and the British military commander in North America had been given clear instructions: "Force should be repelled by force."

There would be no negotiation. There was to be war. The task of the Second Continental Congress was even more difficult than the first: it was to manage a brand-new nation undertaking an armed rebellion.

THE BATTLES OF LEXINGTON AND CONCORD

On April 19, 1775, armed colonists (some of them warned by Paul Revere on his famous midnight ride) confronted seven hundred British troops at Lexington, Massachusetts. The British soldiers, or redcoats, were on their way to seize the Americans' military supplies in Concord. The colonists could not stop the British in Lexington, but most of the supplies had been destroyed or hidden before the redcoats reached Concord. On their way back to Boston, the British faced the Americans again at Concord's North Bridge. This time the redcoats were forced to withdraw, returning to Boston under American fire. The day ended with 273 British soldiers and 95 American colonists dead. The American Revolution had officially begun.

Map of the Battles of Lexington and Concord in 1775.

That rebellion began on Wednesday, April 19, 1775. British troops and American colonists clashed in Massachusetts. Jefferson heard the reports. Any "last hopes of reconciliation" were gone. "A frenzy of revenge seems to have seized all ranks of people," he said.

Lord Dunmore, Virginia's governor, took control of the gunpowder in Williamsburg, which left the Virginians disarmed. An angry crowd gathered in front of the Governor's Palace. Furious, Dunmore called the crowd "one of the highest insults, that could be offered to the authority of his majesty's government." He decided that the British government had a natural ally in Virginia—the slaves owned by Virginian colonists. In exchange for their freedom, the slaves might be willing to fight to support the British.

Dunmore made a public offer that was shocking to the wealthy white people of the state: he would "declare freedom to the slaves, and reduce the city of Williamsburg to ashes" if there was any additional "insult or injury" to the authority of the British government.

To Jefferson, Dunmore's behavior showed a larger truth: the British were not going to talk, negotiate, or even consider the demands of their colonies. The bolder the Americans grew, the surlier the British seemed. "A little knowledge of human nature and attention to its ordinary workings," Jefferson remarked, "might have foreseen that the spirits of the people here were in a state in which they were more likely to be provoked than frightened" by actions like Dunmore's.

Amid bloodshed in Massachusetts, struggles over gunpowder in Virginia, and talk of armed slave rebellion, Jefferson left home in June 1775 for Philadelphia, Pennsylvania, to attend the Second Continental Congress.

A painting of the Second Continental Congress in Philadelphia, where delegates from the colonies voted on the Declaration of Independence.

CHAPTER SEVEN

The Famous Mr. Jefferson

As our enemies have found we can reason like men, so let us show them we can fight like men also.
—Thomas Jefferson

Jefferson found himself at home in Philadelphia. In a way, he had been preparing for this moment all his life. There had been the glittering evenings in Fauquier's palace, full of music and ideas; the golden years in the household of George Wythe, where he soaked up law and history; his time as a Virginia politician, learning from men such as Peyton Randolph what it meant to get things done. The Jefferson style—

learning from elders, being pleasant to peers, and using both mind and pen to influence the world—served him well.

In Virginia, Jefferson had known everything and everyone. In Philadelphia, he met new people and new ideas. He was noticed by many. Samuel Ward of Rhode Island remembered seeing "the famous Mr. Jefferson" and said that the Virginian "looks like a very sensible spirited fine fellow and by the pamphlet which he wrote last summer [the *Summary View*] he certainly is one."

Jefferson and all the other members of the Congress listened every day to news and rumors of war. John Adams of Massachusetts proposed that George Washington be appointed the commanding general of the Continental army. Two days later came the second battle of the Revolutionary War, the Battle of Bunker Hill. British and colonial troops clashed in Boston, Massachusetts, and although the British were victorious, they suffered heavy losses.

A depiction of the Battle of Bunker Hill in Boston.

What Jefferson had heard Patrick Henry say in St. John's Church was now fact. There was no peace.

Jefferson found a sense of courage in Philadelphia. "Nobody now entertains a doubt but that we are able to cope with the whole force of Great Britain, if we are but willing to exert ourselves," he wrote. Together with John Dickinson (the author of *Letters from a Farmer in Pennsylvania*), Jefferson wrote *A Declaration of the Causes and Necessity for Taking Up Arms,* defending the rights of Americans to do what they were already doing: fighting the British. The Continental Congress made one last effort to end the violence, sending an "Olive Branch Petition" to the king as a way to avoid any more bloodshed. Nothing came of it. The war must continue.

At gatherings like the Congress, Jefferson rarely spoke out in large groups. He preferred to make his mark in different ways, particularly through the written word. John Adams noticed that Jefferson's reluctance to speak in public served him well. A public speaker, Adams remarked, could hardly avoid making enemies. A man like Jefferson, who would rather work in private with a pen, or negotiate quietly in a small group, could push for what he wanted without much risk of making others angry at him—something Jefferson avoided all his life.

In August 1775, Jefferson left the Congress and returned to his family at Monticello. There, with Patty, he had built the life he had always imagined for himself: dwelling in a beautiful house, surrounded by beautiful things, listening to music whenever possible, with his wife and daughters close and other family nearby. That August, he wrote a letter to one member of that family, his cousin John Randolph. Randolph owned perhaps the best violin in Virginia; Jefferson had envied it for a long time. Randolph was also a Loyalist. Dedicated to the English king, he wanted no part of a rebellion against Great Britain.

Randolph was planning to leave Virginia for England. Jefferson hoped to find a way to make his cousin useful to the American cause, and his letter made it clear what he wanted.

The British, Jefferson said, thought that only "a small faction" of the colonists were angry enough to rebel. "They have taken it into their heads too that we are cowards" and would quickly retreat in the face of force. He wanted Randolph to correct these mistaken ideas and make it clear in England that the cause of rebellion had wide support among Americans, who were determined to fight. If the British had more respect for the Americans as enemies, Jefferson knew, they might be willing to negotiate or yield to American demands.

But Jefferson did not want to leave his cousin with angry words. He parted on a warm note. "My collection of classics and of books . . . is not so complete as I could wish. As you are going to the land of literature and of books you may be willing to dispose of some of yours here and replace them there in better editions." He would be glad to take any books

Randolph felt like parting with. It was a hint that even though they held opposite views on the Revolution, they were both men of culture who shared a love of learning.

John Randolph replied with the same affection. "Though we *may politically* differ in sentiment," he wrote to his cousin, "yet I see no reason why *privately* we may not cherish the same esteem for each other. . . . Should any coolness happen between us, I'll take care not to be the first mover of it."

Jefferson's message to Randolph achieved what he had hoped for. In England, his letter made its way to the British secretary of state for the colonies. He succeeded in making his point to powerful men in the British government: the Americans were not going to give up easily.

Independence Hall in Philadelphia, where the Second Continental Congress met from 1775 to 1781.

Jefferson spent much of September 1775 at Monticello with his family. The time was not happy, however. His daughter Jane, only a year and a half old, died. But he could not stay home for long; with a rebellion under way, he was needed. He returned to the Congress in Philadelphia on September 25.

His mind was on his home, his wife, and his one surviving daughter. He wrote to Patty but heard nothing back from her; she was ill. "I have never received the scrip of a pen from any mortal in Virginia since I left it," he wrote frantically to one of his brothers-in-law, "nor by any enquiries I could make to hear of my family. The suspense under which I am is too terrible to be endured. If anything has happened, for God's sake let me know it."

He was anxious for more than his own family. There were reports of troops and cannons on their way by ship from England to America. One of their targets was Virginia. "The plan is to lay waste all the plantations of our river sides," Jefferson worried.

In October 1775, Jefferson's cousin Peyton Randolph suffered a stroke and died five hours later. Jefferson had adored and admired Randolph; he was stunned and shocked at the loss.

In November, Lord Dunmore followed through on his earlier threat and promised freedom to any slave who took up arms against the American revolutionaries. Frightened white

Virginians believed that their worst nightmares of armed slaves turning against their masters were becoming real.

Jefferson's daughter and his cousin were dead, his wife was ill, and his home was in danger. "We care not for our towns, and the destructions of our houses would not cost us a sigh," a friend wrote from Virginia. "I have long since given up mine as lost." Danger and destruction seemed to press in on Jefferson from all sides as the war continued.

CHAPTER EIGHT

The Course of
Human Events

*The bells rung all day and almost all night. Even the chimers
chimed away.*
— JOHN ADAMS, DESCRIBING THE REACTION IN
PHILADELPHIA TO THE DECLARATION OF INDEPENDENCE

About seven o'clock in the morning of Sunday, March 31,
1776, Thomas Jefferson's mother, fifty-five years old, had
a stroke and died within an hour. Jane Randolph Jefferson
was buried at Monticello. Jefferson made certain his mother
would always be part of his home, and part of him.

Already struggling to win a revolution and create a new

form of government, Jefferson was brought face to face with a deep personal crisis. He often suffered from a headache at times of emotional distress, one so severe he was "obliged to avoid reading, writing, and almost thinking." That headache had plagued him in the wake of his heartbreak over Rebecca Burwell. With the death of his mother, the blood and nerves in his brain gave him nothing but suffering. The force of her death was almost more than he could stand. The pain would not stop.

It was a strange time for Jefferson. He lived with his headache, his grief, and his uncertainty about his country's fate. But he also belonged to the world outside Monticello. He left home in May, arriving in Philadelphia seven days later. Patty stayed behind in Virginia. "I am here in the same uneasy anxious state in which I was the last fall without Mrs. Jefferson who could not come with me," Jefferson said.

At first, he felt out of place in Philadelphia. The other members of the Congress were all talking of matters he had missed while he had been in Virginia. But he soon found himself at the center of everything.

At the end of the first week in June, a representative of the Congress proposed that the "United Colonies" were free of "all allegiance to the British Crown, and that all political connection between them and the state of Great Britain is, and ought to be, totally dissolved."

For more than a year, the Americans had been at war with

Britain. But they had not formally declared themselves to be a new, independent country, rather than subjects of Great Britain fighting for their rights. The hour of decision was now at hand. The debate over independence began the next day.

John Adams, George Wythe, and others argued that the time had come for Americans to form their own country. Other representatives worried that declaring their independence from England too early might provoke some, if not all, of the colonies to abandon the American cause. If that happened, Jefferson reported, the Americans would have a difficult time finding any foreign allies who would support them.

Finally, a compromise was reached. The members decided that New York, New Jersey, Pennsylvania, Delaware, Maryland, and South Carolina were not yet ready for independence. "It was thought most prudent to wait a while for them," Jefferson said. But not too long. A vote was scheduled for three weeks later, in the beginning of July. In the meantime, committees were appointed to draft a declaration of independence, prepare a plan for the new government, and set guidelines for negotiating with foreign countries.

But who should write the declaration? John Adams thought it should be Thomas Jefferson.

Adams and Jefferson could hardly have been more different. Adams was a New Englander, Thomas Jefferson a Virginian. Adams was eight years older and about five inches shorter. He had difficulty holding his tongue or his temper;

A portrait of John Adams painted by Mather Brown while Jefferson and Adams were in Europe in the 1780s.

Jefferson was a master of keeping his emotions in check. But the two of them formed one of the greatest and most complicated alliances in American history. "I consider you and him as the North and South Poles of the American Revolution," a friend once wrote to Adams. "Some talked, some wrote, and some fought to promote and establish it, but you and Mr. Jefferson *thought* for us all."

"Mr. Jefferson came into Congress in June, 1775, and brought with him a reputation for literature, science and a happy talent of composition," John Adams himself wrote later, explaining how the responsibility for the declaration had fallen upon Jefferson. "Writings of his were handed about. . . . Though a silent member of Congress, he was so prompt, frank, explicit and decisive upon committees and in conversation . . . that he soon seized upon my heart; and upon this occasion I gave him my vote."

As Adams remembered it, Jefferson at first suggested that Adams himself should be the writer of a declaration of independence from Great Britain.

"I will not," Adams said.

"You should do it," Jefferson argued.

"Oh! No."

"Why will you not? You ought to do it."

"I will not."

"Why?"

"Reasons enough."

"What can be your reasons?" Jefferson demanded.

"Reason first, you are a Virginian, and a Virginian ought to appear at the head of this business," Adams responded. "Reason second, I am obnoxious, suspected, and unpopular. You are very much otherwise. Reason third, you can write ten times better than I can."

"Well, if you are decided, I will do as well as I can."

"Very well. When you have drawn it up, we will have a meeting."

Thomas Jefferson, Benjamin Franklin, John Adams, Roger Sherman, and Robert Livingston were on the committee responsible for producing the Declaration of Independence. This painting portrays Franklin, Adams, and Jefferson.

Jefferson began drafting the Declaration of Independence while staying in a small suite at the house of bricklayer Jacob Graff in Philadelphia.

꙳ ꙳

Thomas Jefferson sat down to write the declaration in a three-story house owned by the bricklayer Jacob Graff. He slept in one room and wrote in a private parlor across the stairs, on a small wooden desk that he had designed himself.

Jefferson knew what had to be done, and he knew how to do it. His purpose, he said, was "not to find out new principles, or new arguments, never before thought of . . . but to place before mankind the common sense of the subject." What he wrote was "intended to be an expression of the American mind," and he argued that self-government was part of the nature of things. The declaration began:

> When in the course of human events it becomes necessary for one people to dissolve the political bands which have connected them with another, and to assume among the powers of the earth the separate and equal station to which the laws of nature and nature's God entitle them, a decent respect to the opinions of mankind requires that they should declare the causes which impel them to the separation.
>
> We hold these truths to be self-evident: that all men are created equal; that they are endowed by their creator with certain unalienable rights; that among these are life, liberty and the pursuit of happiness; that to secure these rights, governments are instituted among men, deriving

their just powers from the consent of the governed; that whenever any form of government becomes destructive of these ends, it is the right of the people to alter or to abolish it, and to institute new government, laying its foundation on such principles, and organizing its powers in such form, as to them shall seem most likely to effect their safety and happiness.

THE DECLARATION OF INDEPENDENCE

Thomas Jefferson's Declaration of Independence not only laid out the reasons the United States wanted to separate itself from England but also made clear new and remarkable theories about government and power. In it, Thomas Jefferson announced that emperors, kings, and noblemen do not have the right to rule others simply because of their birth. Instead, he claimed, true power lies in the people who are governed.

In modern language, the introduction to the declaration says:

Sometimes one country has to break its political connections with another so that it can become independent and equal to other nations. (It is entitled to do this under the laws of nature and of God.) To show respect for what others may think, the people of that country should announce why they are forced to separate.

We claim that the following facts are obviously true: that all men are created equal; that they are given certain rights by God that can never be taken away, including the rights to life, liberty, and the search for happiness. People create governments to protect these rights, and the powers of these governments are granted by the people they govern. If any government destroys, rather than protects, these rights, the people can change that government or remove it from power and create a new one. This new government should be based on the ideas and organized in the ways that the people believe will be most likely to guarantee them safety and happiness.

The "original rough draft" of the Declaration of Independence, handwritten by Jefferson.

Benjamin Franklin, whose wide-ranging interests reflected Jefferson's own.

The declaration went on to make clear America's complaints against England, and Jefferson spared nothing in his attacks on George III. John Adams and Benjamin Franklin read his draft and offered suggestions. Congress read what Jefferson had written and began to debate it on July 1, 1776.

Jefferson hated being edited by such a large group. He fairly writhed as he sat in the Pennsylvania State House, listening to member after member offering his thoughts, wanting to change this or cut that. South Carolina and Georgia objected to the sections against the slave trade, which were cut. Others thought Jefferson's attacks on England were too bitter, and those were taken out as well. But in the end, they voted for what Jefferson had written. The Declaration of Independence was adopted by the Second Continental Congress on July 2, 1776.

Two days later, on the fourth of July, the Congress met to give the document its final approval. Horseflies from a nearby stable buzzed through the Pennsylvania State House, biting the legs of the representatives through their silk stockings. They swatted at the flies with their handkerchiefs, but with little success, and became impatient to get the business over with. They did. The declaration was finally, formally approved. The United States of America was its own country at last.

On the following Monday, the news was announced in Philadelphia in front of the State House. The crowd cheered, "God bless the free states of North America!"

Stone engraving of the Declaration of Independence, signed by the Second Continental Congress.

CHAPTER NINE

The Pull of Duty

I pray you to come. I am under a sacred obligation to go home.
—THOMAS JEFFERSON

In 1776, with Jefferson at work in Philadelphia, Patty suffered a disastrous miscarriage. In the same days and weeks in which he wrote the Declaration of Independence, Jefferson could not rest easy about his wife. "I wish I could be better satisfied on the point of Patty's recovery," he wrote to a brother-in-law. It was his duty to stay in Philadelphia, but he longed to be at home with his family.

He could not leave. If he did, Virginia would not have the correct number of representatives in the Congress. He asked his friend Richard Henry Lee of Virginia to come and take his place, but until that happened, he had to wait. Hard at work, Jefferson wrote a proposed constitution for the state of Virginia and suggested rules for how members of Congress should debate laws. "No Member shall read any printed paper in the House," he advised. "When the House is sitting no Member shall speak [or whisper] to another as to interrupt any Member who may be speaking in Debate."

The war dragged on, with victory for the Americans nowhere in sight. It was difficult for the Continental army to recruit enough soldiers. "Our camps recruit slowly, amazingly slowly," Jefferson noticed. "God knows in what it will end."

Word came of a plot within the army to kill George Washington, and of attacks by Cherokees, allied with the British, on American forces to the south. Depressed and anxious, Jefferson could find little good news.

In the fall, Jefferson returned at last to Monticello, relieved to be with his wife and daughter again. Patsy celebrated her fourth birthday with her father in September.

Jefferson did not leave again for Philadelphia. He chose to settle in Williamsburg to work on creating a government for the brand-new state of Virginia, taking his family with him. When not at work, he could spend his hours with Patty and Patsy. It was perfect.

In writing the Declaration of Independence, Jefferson had laid out sweeping ideas for a new form of government based on freedom. Now he was learning how to translate those ideas into action by transforming the laws of Virginia. To make the philosophy of the declaration into the politics of state law, he brought bills to the General Assembly. The House of Burgesses was no more; the new assembly would debate bills and create laws for Virginia.

To achieve his ends, Jefferson needed to talk to others, change their minds, and convince them to vote with him. He needed power, and he began to figure out how to get it.

Jefferson started carefully, introducing bills in order to test whether Virginians were ready for change. Finding that they were, he pressed ahead. His first major bill was an attack on the laws and customs governing inheritance, which had forced large landowners to leave all their property to a single heir, usually the eldest son. This practice, Jefferson (an eldest son and heir himself) believed, created an aristocratic class, wealthy and privileged. That was something a brand-new democracy did not need.

Jefferson's other bills reformed the justice system by ending the harshest punishments and limiting the death penalty to murder and treason. He created a system of public education and made it easier for immigrants to become citizens.

As he worked, Jefferson took note of a newcomer to the political scene: James Madison. Madison was twenty-five;

Jefferson was thirty-three. Madison was small; Jefferson was tall. Madison was quiet and understated; Jefferson was given to grand pronouncements.

James Madison was to become Thomas Jefferson's most trusted advisor. Born in 1751 to a wealthy family of tobacco farmers, Madison had gone north to be educated at the College of New Jersey (later to become Princeton). Jefferson admired Madison's intelligence, his elegant speech, his self-command, and his gentle manners.

James Madison was Jefferson's closest political confidant. He often protected Jefferson from making exaggerated public statements during heated moments.

Madison and Jefferson cooperated on a project to extend religious freedom in Virginia. Jefferson was highly skeptical of the idea that belief in any religion should be enforced by law. It took many years, but eventually Virginia's laws were changed. Freedom of religion would be offered to, in Jefferson's words, "the Jew and the Gentile, the Christian and Mahometan [Muslim], the Hindoo, and infidel of every denomination."

As a lawmaker, Jefferson tackled another issue as emotional and as difficult as religion: slavery. He and his allies proposed a law to free all slaves "born after a certain day." The bill also required "deportation at a proper age." Freed slaves, in Jefferson's vision, were to be returned to Africa.

The bill did not become law. Years later, Jefferson wrote about the struggle. "It was found that the public mind would not yet bear the proposition [of ending slavery], nor will it bear it even at this day." But he foresaw clearly that slavery would not last forever in America and that his fellow Virginians were only putting off the day when the injustice would have to be faced.

"Nothing is more certainly written in the book of fate, than that these people are to be free," he predicted. But the vision of human beings of different races living together in peace was beyond him. "Two races, equally free, cannot live in the same government," he wrote.

Whether there would truly be a government for people of any race in North America was uncertain as 1776 came to an end. George Washington's army did what it could, but the chance of victory looked faint.

Jefferson continued his work in the Virginia General Assembly over the winter and spring before moving his family back to Monticello. In May 1777, Patty gave birth to a son, who lived only seventeen days. If the Jeffersons gave him a name, it has not survived in any record. A bit more than a year later, on August 1, 1778, Patty gave birth to another daughter, named Mary but always called Polly.

Worries about the war were everywhere. The good news was that King Louis XVI of France had become an ally of the

Americans, sending a force of six thousand soldiers to fight alongside George Washington's army. The violence, however, was moving farther south. Amid growing concern in 1779 that the British would soon try to conquer Virginia, Thomas Jefferson was elected the state's governor for a term of one year.

The Governor's Palace in Williamsburg, where young Thomas Jefferson had spent so much time as a guest, was now to be his. He was thirty-six, a husband, a father, the governor of Virginia, and a statesman of the United States of America.

Before Jefferson became governor, Virginia had seen very little of the war's violence. That was about to change. Georgia had collapsed after the British took the city of Savannah, and South Carolina would be next. Virginia would soon be under threat from British troops from the east and from British soldiers and their Native American allies in the West.

In the spring of 1780, Jefferson moved the capital of Virginia to Richmond, believing that the new city, farther from the sea, would be easier to defend. He saw danger everywhere. "While we are threatened with a formidable attack from the northward on our Ohio settlements and from the southern Indians on our frontiers," Jefferson said, "our eastern country is exposed to invasion from the British army in Carolina." Elected to a second yearlong term as governor in 1780, Jefferson had no relief from bad news.

An attack on Virginia came in December 1780, led by Benedict Arnold, once an American general, now a traitor who had sold himself to the British. Word reached the capital, Richmond, on New Year's Day 1781.

Jefferson was slow to take the report seriously. He had already heard many rumors of invasion that had turned out to be false. He waited to be sure before he called out the militia, men who were not full-time soldiers but were trained to fight in an emergency. As it turned out, he waited too long.

On January 5, Jefferson's slaves Robert Hemings and James Hemings drove Patty and the rest of the Jefferson family out of the city, to another home Jefferson owned west of the capital. On that very afternoon, the British troops arrived in Richmond and fired cannonballs into the city. "In ten minutes not a white man was to be seen in Richmond; they ran hard as they could" to a camp of American soldiers nearby, recalled Isaac Granger Jefferson.

The British had brought along handcuffs, hoping to capture the author of the Declaration of Independence. But Thomas Jefferson had fled the city. Soldiers reached his house and asked where the governor was. "He's gone to the mountains," George Granger, Isaac's father, told them, protecting his master.

"Where is the keys to the house?" the officer asked. Isaac's father handed over the keys.

Benedict Arnold, an American general turned traitor, in 1781.

"Where is the silver?" the officer asked.

"It was all sent up to the mountains," George Granger answered. It was a lie. As Isaac recalled it, his father had "put all the silver about the house in a bed tick [mattress] and hid it under a bed in the kitchen and saved it too."

The British seized a large number of Jefferson's slaves, including Isaac Granger Jefferson. As they were marched out of Richmond, they heard the sounds of war—one blast, Isaac remembered, was "like an earthquake." (The slaves were held for a time by the British and finally managed to return to Monticello after the war ended. Jefferson was, Isaac remembered, relieved to see them again, and also relieved to hear that his silver had been saved.) By waiting to activate the militia, Jefferson made the common political mistake of following the people rather than leading them. From this setback, he learned that as a leader, he must be more decisive.

Isaac Granger Jefferson, a slave at Monticello, left a valuable oral history of life in Jefferson's household.

CHAPTER TEN

Redcoats at Monticello

Such terror and confusion you have no idea of. Governor,
Council, everybody scampering.
—BETSY AMBLER, DAUGHTER OF REBECCA BURWELL

Jefferson's Virginia was teetering in the face of British force.
Governor Jefferson and the General Assembly retreated to
Charlottesville, but they could barely collect enough people
to get the business of government done.

In this difficult period, Thomas and Patty Jefferson went
through an all-too-familiar tragedy: the death of yet another
child. Lucy Elizabeth, not quite six months old, died on an

April morning in 1781. She was their third child to die. Only Patsy and Polly were still living.

Jefferson chose to stay with Patty the day after Lucy's death. "There being nothing that I know of very pressing," he wrote to his fellow politicians, "and Mrs. Jefferson in a situation in which I would not wish to leave her, I shall not attend today."

In May, British troops (called redcoats for their bright uniforms) were advancing across Virginia, and there seemed to be no way of stopping them. On Saturday, June 2, Jefferson and the other lawmakers had gathered at Monticello. They did not realize that British troops were on their way. Jack Jouett, a Virginia militiaman, saw the British soldiers as they rode and realized that they intended to capture Jefferson.

Jouett saddled his horse for a daring nighttime ride of forty miles. Galloping over woodlands and along ridges, Jouett stayed clear of the main roads, hoping to avoid the enemy. One witness said that his face was "cruelly lashed by tree-branches as he rode forward," leaving "scars which are said to have remained the rest of his life." The British stopped to rest for a few hours around eleven, giving Jouett a bit more time.

Jouett arrived at Monticello just before dawn and told Jefferson of the danger. Calmly, Jefferson ordered breakfast, summoned a carriage for his family, and prepared to leave his home. Patty and the two children went to seek safety at a nearby plantation. The other Virginia lawmakers returned to Charlottesville, leaving Jefferson and a few slaves alone at Monticello.

The slaves hid the silver. Jefferson collected what papers and documents he could. Then he decided to see things for himself. Taking a spyglass, he climbed to the peak of a nearby mountain and looked at the road to Charlottesville. He saw nothing out of the ordinary and turned to go. But as he did so, he realized that his sword cane had slipped to the ground. As he picked it up again, his curiosity got the better of him. He peered through the glass.

It was then that he saw the British.

Back at Monticello, Jefferson mounted his best horse, Caractacus, and took off after his family. The redcoats arrived five minutes later. One cocked a pistol and aimed it at the chest of Martin Hemings, one of Jefferson's slaves. He demanded to be told where Jefferson was, or he would fire. "Fire away, then," Hemings said.

The soldier did not shoot. Martin Hemings escaped with his life, and so did Jefferson.

The governor's reputation was another matter.

On Tuesday, June 12, 1781, the General Assembly of Virginia gave Jack Jouett a pair of pistols and a sword, in gratitude for his brave ride through darkness. It also passed a resolution to investigate Jefferson's behavior as governor during the previous year.

Jefferson was mortified. He had been in charge while Virginia was invaded and while the state government and the governor himself had been forced to flee from British troops. The inquiry did not last long, and the assembly ended up approving of Jefferson's actions. But he felt the sting of the accusations so sharply that he thought of quitting politics for good.

In October 1781, the Americans defeated the British at the Battle of Yorktown in Virginia. When the commander of the British forces surrendered to George Washington, the Revolutionary War came to an end. It would seem that Thomas Jefferson should have been elated. His country had won; his cause had triumphed.

The British invasion of Virginia from 1780 to 1781 ended with the American triumph at Yorktown.

But Jefferson could not share fully in the joy. He believed himself a failure and could not let go of worries that the public would believe he had been guilty of "treasons of the heart and not mere weakness of the head." The attacks on his service as governor "had inflicted a wound on my spirit which will only be cured by the all-healing grave."

His spirit was suffering from another wound as well. Patty had given birth to their sixth child, a daughter they named Lucy Elizabeth after her sister who had died. Patty's life was in danger. "She has been ever since," Jefferson wrote to a friend, "and still continues, very dangerously ill."

By the summer of 1782, Patty could not leave her bed. Her husband "was never out of calling," their daughter Patsy recalled. Either beside her bed or in a small room next door, he stayed nearby. Patty longed for his company. "Her eyes ever rested on him, ever followed him," their family remembered. "When he spoke, no other sound could reach her ear or attract her attention. When she waked from slumber, she looked momentarily alarmed and distressed, and even appeared to be frightened" if her husband was not in sight.

On Friday, September 6, the end came. Several of Monticello's slaves, including Elizabeth Hemings, stood around the bed, and Thomas Jefferson sat by his wife as she told him her last wishes. "When she came to the children, she wept and could not speak for some time. Finally she held up her hand and . . . told him she could not die happy if she thought her . . . children were ever to have a stepmother brought in over them."

Patty's own mother had died when she was young, and she had grown up with two step-mothers, one after the other. It seemed that she did not want her daughters—Patsy, who was nearly ten; Polly, four years old; and Lucy, still a baby—to have the same experience.

Jefferson promised Patty he would never marry again. Among the witnesses to that pledge was Eliza-beth Hemings's daughter Sally, Patty's half sister. She was not quite ten years old.

On her deathbed, Jefferson's wife was said to have given this servant bell to Sally Hemings.

➜︎ ➜︎

Patty's death was almost more than Jefferson could bear. "The violence of his emotion, when, almost by stealth, I en-tered his room by night, to this day I dare not describe to myself," his daughter Patsy wrote fifty years later. In their grief, Patsy clung to her father, and he to her. "I was never a moment from his side," she remembered. Jefferson could not stand to be still, and he walked and rode on horseback for hours, with Patsy close by. "In those melancholy rambles I was his constant companion—a solitary witness to many a burst of grief," she wrote.

Patty was buried at Monticello. Jefferson chose a Greek quotation from Homer for her tombstone, along with a simple and painful inscription in English:

To the memory of
Martha Jefferson,
Daughter of John Wayles;
Born October 19th, 1748, O.S.
Intermarried with
Thomas Jefferson
January 1st, 1772;
Torn from him by death
September 6th, 1782:
This monument of his love is inscribed.

CHAPTER ELEVEN

A Struggle for Respect

The states will go to war with each other in defiance of Congress; one will call in France to her assistance; another Great Britain, and so we shall have all the wars of Europe brought to our own doors.
—THOMAS JEFFERSON

He was nearly forty years old, and he had never really failed at anything. A favored son, a brilliant student, a lawmaker of his state at the age of twenty-five, the author of the *Summary View* at thirty-one and of the Declaration of Independence at thirty-three, the governor of Virginia at thirty-six, Thomas Jefferson was accustomed to public success and praise.

No longer. His beloved wife had died. His performance as governor had been publicly criticized. As a leader, Jefferson proved to be less than what the people wanted. It was a fact Jefferson hated, but it was a fact nonetheless.

Jefferson had to come to terms with the idea that a life lived in public would mean criticism, attacks, and even hatred. The only way to avoid this would be to return to Monticello and live in private. That was not a choice he was willing to make. In the summer following Patty's death, Jefferson was elected to Congress. He was no longer helplessly lost in grief; he was ready to engage with the world once more.

Jefferson traveled north to join a national government that had little actual power. There was no president or Supreme Court. Congress could pass laws but had no way to enforce them. It could not tax the states, make rules about trade, or create an army or a navy. Each of the thirteen states basically governed itself.

Congress did not even have a safe place to meet. In June 1783, the lawmakers were driven out of Philadelphia when three hundred former soldiers of the Continental army rose in revolt, demanding their pay. The members of Congress, on the run from their own people, fled the city for Princeton, New Jersey. They stayed there until November, when they moved to Annapolis, Maryland.

Jefferson worried that without a strong national government to hold the states together, civil war was likely. What was to stop one state from turning on another? What would hold this new democracy together?

Congress's first and most important task was to approve the treaty that would formally end the Revolutionary War. The task was difficult because not all the members of Congress had traveled to Annapolis. Nine states needed to be represented, and only six were present. "We have some hopes of Rhode Island coming in today, but when two more will be added" seemed as unknowable "as when the next earthquake will happen," Jefferson wrote. When representatives from Connecticut and New Jersey at last arrived, the treaty was approved.

Jefferson wrote a proclamation to announce the news. He called on "all the good citizens of these states" to draw on "that good faith which is every man's surest guide" and accept the terms of the treaty. The author of the Declaration of Independence had declared the peace.

The peace did not seem perfectly secure, however. Jefferson worried that Great Britain had not given up all hope of controlling North America. "I find they have subscribed a very large sum of money in England for exploring the country from the Mississippi to California," he wrote in December 1783. "They pretend it is only to promote knowledge. I am afraid they have thoughts of colonizing in that quarter. Some of us have been talking here in a feeble way of making the attempt to search that country." Jefferson liked the idea of exploring the West, although he was not sure how to pay for it. "But I doubt whether we have enough of that kind of spirit to raise the money."

Jefferson would always be fascinated by the American West. He loved the image of endless forests and was eager to learn more of the animals that lived and used to live there, particularly "the different species of bones, teeth, and tusks of the Mammoth."

A scientist as well as a politician, Jefferson devoured news of manned balloon flights, comets, and archaeological discoveries in Siberia.

These upper jawbones of a North American mastodon, found in Kentucky, were part of Jefferson's fossil collection.

He thought his daughter Patsy should also improve her mind. Patsy stayed in Philadelphia while her father was in Annapolis. (The two younger children, Polly and Lucy, lived with their mother's relatives in Virginia.) Jefferson hired a French tutor for Patsy, asked her to read novels in French and Spanish, and informed her that he expected her to make progress in her studies. Her learning, he told her, "will render you more worthy of my love."

He gave Patsy direction on how to spend her days, telling her that "the following is what I should approve":

- *From 8 to 10 o'clock, practice music.*
- *From 10 to 1, dance one day and draw another.*
- *From 1 to 2, draw on the day you dance, and write a letter the next day.*
- *From 3 to 4, read French.*
- *From 4 to 5, exercise yourself in music.*
- *From 5 till bed-time, read English, write, etc.*

Jefferson may have been able to control how his daughter spent her days, but he could control little about the situation in Congress. It was difficult even to keep enough members together to allow the assembly to vote. "I suppose the crippled state of Congress is not new to you," Jefferson wrote to George Washington. "We are wasting our time and labor in vain efforts to do business."

Jefferson worried that the weakness of Congress might lead to his worst fear: that the United States would once more become subject to England. After reading a report from Benjamin Franklin, Jefferson wrote to Washington that "though they have made peace with us," the British were not happy with the fact that they had lost control of their former colony. The belief in England that the states were quarreling among themselves, and that "the people here are already fatigued [tired] with their new government," might lead Great Britain to try to regain its hold over America.

In May 1784, Jefferson accepted a new task for Congress. He was to travel to France, America's ally in the Revolutionary War, as an ambassador of the United States government. Patsy would go with him, as well as his slave James Hemings; he wanted Hemings to be trained as a French cook.

On July 5, Jefferson, with his daughter and his slave, left Boston Harbor, a man of the New World bound for the Old. The voyage across the Atlantic was swift and pleasant; Patsy always remembered the "good company and . . . excellent table" on board the ship.

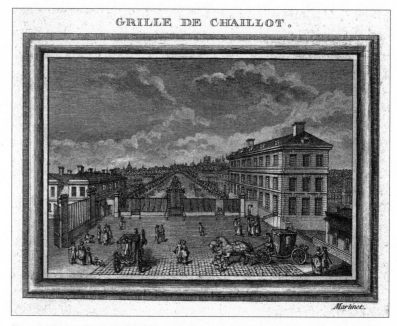

GRILLE DE CHAILLOT.

Martinet

The neighborhood of one of Jefferson's Paris homes.

Jefferson was in love with France before he even reached Paris. By the time he got there, he was already convinced that France was "the most agreeable country on earth." But even amid the high fashion and the high-flown talk, Jefferson never forgot to put America's best interests first. He was determined to help his brand-new nation take its place as an equal with the older countries of Europe, and he believed it was necessary that the United States keep up a strong alliance with France in order to resist threats from England.

While in France, Jefferson negotiated treaties on whale oil and tobacco, fighting for the interests of American sailors and farmers. He kept a wary eye on a French expedition to the South Seas, worrying that perhaps the voyage was intended to give the French a foothold on the west coast of North America. Above all, he worked to maintain a relationship with the French government that would keep England in check.

Jefferson also made sure that Patsy had the fashionable clothes she needed for life in a European capital. She attended boarding school at a convent, "a house of education altogether the best in France, and at which the best masters attend," Jefferson said. For himself, Jefferson found a house called the Hôtel Lândron and paid for wine, furniture, music, and horses out of his own pocket while waiting for his salary to arrive from the United States. "For the articles of household furniture, clothes, and a carriage . . . I have been obliged to anticipate my salary from which however I shall never be able to repay it," Jefferson wrote to James Monroe. He wanted his friend to mention the fact to Congress but to do so carefully to avoid offending anyone. "I'd rather be ruined in my fortunes, than in their esteem," he added.

His fellow congressman John Adams was also in Paris, with his wife, Abigail, and their family. Jefferson admired the Adamses' house; Abigail found Jefferson charming. "Mr. Adams's colleague Mr. Jefferson is an excellent man," she wrote.

The Paris in which Jefferson and Adams lived and worked was in the midst of enormous growth. The city was "every day enlarging and beautifying," Jefferson said. There were houses, theaters, cafés, gambling parlors, stalls where books were for sale. Jefferson loved it. He learned all he could about the architecture, the art, the theater, the music, the literature, the food, the wine, and the people of this "great and good" country.

"So ask the travelled inhabitant of any nation," he wrote later, "in what country on earth would you rather live?" The first answer, of course, would be one's own. But the second? France, always France.

〽 〼

As Jefferson worked to make it clear in Europe that the United States was a country to be respected, he faced a crisis on the seas. The Barbary States—Morocco, Algiers, Tunis, and Tripoli—were threatening American ships and the goods that they carried. These four countries were seen as outlaw states that demanded payment from other nations and left those that refused to pay on their own to face murderous pirates in the Mediterranean Sea.

Many European nations paid tribute to the Barbary States to protect their ships. Jefferson had been trying to find out how much these countries gave "to purchase their peace." No one was willing to tell him an exact amount, but it seemed to be between $100,000 and $300,000 a year. "Surely our people will not give this," he wrote to James Monroe. "Would it not be better to offer them an equal treaty? If they refuse, why not go to war with them?"

There were suspicions that England was encouraging pirates to attack American ships. "It is said that Great Britain has encouraged the piratical states to attack our vessels. If this could be proved, I should prefer a war against her [England], rather than against Algiers," a friend of Jefferson's wrote him

America was engaged in almost constant battles with Barbary pirates in the Mediterranean Sea. Jefferson dealt with this issue throughout his service in France, his years as secretary of state, and his two terms as president.

from South Carolina. "But it is a melancholy fact that we are not in a condition to go to war with anybody." The United States government did not have the money to raise an army or a navy or to carry out a war.

🔻 🔻

In January 1785, painful news arrived for Jefferson. His youngest daughter, Lucy, left with her aunt and uncle, had died. Her cousin, also named Lucy, had perished as well. "A most unfortunate whooping cough has deprived you, and us of two sweet Lucys, within a week," Jefferson's sister-in-law wrote to him. Her husband wrote also, telling Jefferson that the girls "both suffered as much pain, indeed more than ever I saw two of their ages experience. . . . They were beyond the reach of medicine."

Jefferson now had only two daughters left alive: Patsy, with him in Paris, and Polly, still with her aunt and uncle. He begged his sister-in-law to "kiss my dear, dear Polly for me. Oh! Could I do it myself!"

Lucy's death made the gloom and damp of a Paris winter even harder to endure. By spring, Jefferson had made a decision: he wanted his family together. With Lucy gone, he was eager to have Polly join him and Patsy in France. "I must have Polly," Jefferson wrote to his brother-in-law in May 1785. "Is there any woman in Virginia [who] could be hired to come?"

CHAPTER TWELVE
His Head and His Heart

We have no rose without its thorn.
—THOMAS JEFFERSON

Jefferson found the shopping in France wonderful. He bought silver and china and wine, along with a new invention—matches. He purchased three dozen of these to send to friends in America. Then there were tickets to the opera, to Italian comedy, to musical performances. And, finally, paintings. Jefferson bought more than sixty in his first five years in Paris. He also chose a sculptor to create a statue of George Washington in Richmond, Virginia's new capital.

The Palace of Versailles.

He attended balls, visited the Palace of Versailles, and made time to see Patsy at her school. "I need not tell you what pleasure it gives me to see you improve in everything agreeable and useful," he wrote to her. He traveled to a school for the blind to learn what he could about its methods of teaching. He tried to play chess but did not have much success. "I have heard them say that when, on his arrival in Paris, he was introduced into a chess club, he was beaten at one, and that so rapidly . . . that he gave up all competition," one of his granddaughters remembered years later. Jefferson was not a man who liked to lose.

He loved Paris, although it was not home. "I am savage enough to prefer the woods, the wilds, and the independence of Monticello, to all the brilliant pleasures of this gay capital," he admitted. Jefferson was liked by the French as well. "He is everything that is good, upright, enlightened, and clever," the Marquis de Lafayette wrote, "and is respected and beloved by everyone that knows him." A hero of the Revolutionary War, Lafayette had fought on the American side and had helped to convince King Louis XVI to support the American cause.

But one person very close to Jefferson did not know him very well. That was his own daughter Polly, who had often been separated from her father as he traveled to Williamsburg, to Philadelphia, to Annapolis, and then to France. A simple letter arrived in Paris for Jefferson. "Dear Papa," Polly wrote to her father, "I want very much to see you and sister Patsy, but you must come to Uncle Eppes's house."

Jefferson wrote back, trying to convince his young daughter that she would like living with him and her sister in Paris better than she imagined. "I wish so much to see you that I have desired your uncle and aunt to send you to me," he told her.

Portrait of the Marquis de Lafayette. He and Jefferson grew extremely close when Jefferson was in France, and Lafayette supported the Americans in the Revolutionary War.

I know, my dear Polly, how sorry you will be, and ought to be, to leave them and your cousins but your sister and myself cannot live without you. . . . In the meantime, you shall be taught here to play on the harpsichord, to draw, to dance, to read and talk French and such other things as will make you more worth of the love of your friends. But above all things, by our care and love of you, we will teach you to love us more than you will do if you stay so far from us.

⋙ ⋘

His younger daughter was not the only person Thomas Jefferson wanted to love him. Sixteen years younger than Jefferson, Maria Cosway was beautiful, "golden-haired, languishing . . . graceful . . . and highly accomplished, especially in music." Jefferson met her and her husband while visiting two Parisian architects and was immediately charmed. He had plans to dine that evening with a duchess, but he sent an excuse so that he could spend it with Maria, her husband, and a friend.

Day after day, as August gave way to September, Jefferson found ways to see Maria. The two wandered along the banks of the Seine and explored hidden gardens. But it could not last forever. Maria had to return home to England. "It will be with infinite pleasure I shall remember the charming days we have passed to-

Portrait of Maria Cosway, to whom Jefferson wrote his most intimate letter, one in which his head and his heart debated openly.

gether," she wrote in a good-bye letter to Jefferson.

Missing her painfully, Jefferson sat down once she had gone to write her a letter, which turned into an essay. He created a dialogue between his heart and his head, his emotions and his logic.

> HEAD: *Well, friend, you seem to be in a pretty trim [in terrible shape].*
>
> HEART: *I am indeed the most wretched of earthly beings. . . .*
>
> HEAD: *. . . This is one of the scrapes into which you are ever leading us. . . .*

The Head scolds the Heart for loving others too much when that love is bound to lead to pain.

> HEAD: *. . . The most effectual [effective] means of being secure against pain is to retire within ourselves, and to suffice for our own happiness. . . . A friend dies or leaves us: we feel as if a limb was cut off. He is sick: we must watch over him, and participate of [in] his pains. . . . He loses a child, a parent, or a partner: we must mourn the loss as if it was our own.*

But the Heart insists that loving someone is worth the price.

> HEART: *. . . In short, my friend, as far as my recollection serves me, I do not know that I ever did a good thing on*

your suggestion, or a dirty one without it. . . . We are not immortal ourselves, my friend; how can we expect our enjoyments to be so? We have no rose without its thorn.

Who wins, the Head or the Heart? Jefferson does not make it entirely clear. But he gives the Heart the last word, and also the highest praise he could offer—credit for the American Revolution.

HEART: . . . If our country, when pressed with wrongs at the point of the bayonet, had been governed by its heads instead of its hearts, where should we have been now? Hanging on a gallows. . . . You began to calculate and to compare wealth and numbers: . . . we supplied enthusiasm against wealth and numbers: we put our existence to the hazard, when the hazard seemed against us, and we saved our country.

⟶ ✦

Maria was gone, but someone else arrived. On Tuesday, June 26, 1787, Polly Jefferson, eight years old, arrived in London, where John and Abigail Adams were now staying. A slave from Monticello had been sent with Polly on the voyage. Her name was Sally Hemings, and she was fourteen.

Polly and Sally stayed with the Adamses until Jefferson could arrange for their travel to France. We do not know how Sally felt, arriving in one foreign country and planning to travel to another, but Polly was not happy. She had become fond of the captain of the ship on which she sailed and hated to be separated from him.

Abigail Adams tried to help Polly stop her tears. "I tell her that I did not see her sister cry once," she wrote to Jefferson. "She replies that her sister was older and ought to do better, besides she had her pappa with her." Abigail then attempted to comfort Polly by showing her a picture of her father, but this was of little use, either. "I show her your picture. She says she cannot know it, how should she when she should not know you."

A night of rest did wonders for Polly's homesickness, and Abigail suggested that Jefferson come himself to fetch the little girl and that he bring Patsy with him. But Jefferson was too busy with work and sent a French servant to bring Polly to Paris. Polly was beside herself. "Thrown into all her former distress," she clung to Abigail, who wrote to Jefferson, "She told me this morning that as she had left all her friends in Virginia to come over the ocean to see you, she did think you would have taken the pains to have come here for her, and not have sent a man whom she cannot understand." She added, "I express her own words."

Polly and Sally Hemings at last arrived safely in Paris. Polly did not remember her older sister but thought her father seemed somewhat familiar. Sally had left her mother, Elizabeth Hemings, in Monticello, but in Paris she was reunited with her brother James. The Jefferson family was together again, and so was part of the Hemings family.

Abigail Adams greatly admired Jefferson, but the two friends grew distant when they began to disagree on political questions in the late 1790s.

CHAPTER THIRTEEN
A Treaty in Paris

He desired to bring my mother back to Virginia with him.
—MADISON HEMINGS, SON OF THOMAS JEFFERSON AND
SALLY HEMINGS

In the years that Thomas Jefferson lived in Paris, France was struggling under a heavy debt, partly because of the money it had spent to support the American Revolution. The system of taxes was unjust, with the heaviest burden falling on commoners rather than wealthy nobles and churchmen. Many people lived in poverty. Patsy always remembered the beggars who surrounded the Jeffersons' carriage as they traveled in Paris. Anger was growing.

Painting of the signing of the Constitution at the Constitutional Convention in Philadelphia in 1787.

Jefferson worried about anger at home as well. In Massachusetts, a Revolutionary War veteran had led a revolt that was quickly put down but was still distressing to many. John Adams wrote to his friend in Paris. "Don't be alarmed at the late turbulence in New England," Adams reassured him. "All will be well, and this commotion will terminate in additional strength to the government." Jefferson was relieved. "I can never fear that things will go far wrong where common sense has fair play," he told Adams.

As France edged closer to revolution, America worked on a change for its own government. It had now been more than a decade since the United States had declared its independence. The national government had been struggling for all those years to manage without any real authority. Finally, it was decided that the United States needed a new constitution. In the spring of 1787, the Constitutional Convention gathered in Philadelphia to create one.

Unable to attend, Jefferson followed the news as closely as he could. He admired the men who had been chosen for the task. "It really is an assembly of demigods," he told Adams.

George Washington sent a draft of the Constitution to Jefferson in Paris; Benjamin Franklin did as well. Letters flowed back and forth. "How do you like our new Constitution?" Jefferson wrote to Adams. Jefferson himself approved of the division of the national government into three branches: Congress, to make the laws; the president, to enforce them; and a system of judges and courts, to be sure that the laws themselves followed the Constitution and that they were enforced fairly. He was also glad to see that Congress would be given the power to raise taxes.

But he was worried as well, particularly because the new constitution did not include a specific list of rights that could never be taken away from the American people. He wanted the document to guarantee, among other things, "freedom of religion, freedom of the press . . . and trials by jury."

Always concerned that America would be tempted to return to a system of monarchy, he also wondered if a president might be reelected over and over until his role would be no different from that of a king. Were the delegates to the Constitutional Convention too worried about violence, such as the kind that had lately arisen in Massachusetts? Could that tempt them to give a president kinglike powers in order to ensure peace?

"We have had 13 states independent 11 years," he pointed out. "There has been one rebellion. . . . Let them take arms. The remedy is to set them right as to facts, pardon and pacify them. What signify a few lives lost? . . . The tree of liberty must be refreshed from time to time with the blood of patriots and tyrants. . . . Our Convention has been too much impressed by the insurrection [rebellion] in Massachusetts."

An illustration of two men fighting during Shays' Rebellion. Daniel Shays, a Revolutionary War veteran, helped raise a militia in protest of state government taxes, which were considered unfair.

However, Jefferson was willing to accept the new Constitution since representatives elected by the people had voted on it. "It is my principle that the will of the majority should always prevail," he told James Madison. He later wrote, "There are indeed some faults . . . but we must be contented to travel on towards perfection, step by step."

Jefferson dreamed of an ideal government that would balance the necessary authority with personal liberty, but he also knew something worthwhile when he saw it. He would not let his vision of a perfect future sabotage the good that might be achieved in the present. "The ground of liberty is to be gained by inches," he once wrote to a friend. "We must be contented to secure what we can get from time to time, and eternally press forward for what is yet to get."

As summer turned to fall, George Washington was chosen to be the first president of the United States under its new constitution. John Adams, the vice president, proposed that Washington should be addressed as "His Highness the President of the United States and protector of their liberties." Jefferson found the title absurd—"the most superlatively ridiculous thing I ever heard of"—and was relieved when the idea failed. It proved, he said, that his

Portrait of John Adams
by Alonzo Chappel.

friend Adams was exactly what Benjamin Franklin had once called him: "always an honest man, often a great one, but sometimes absolutely mad."

Calling the president His Highness might have been foolish but harmless; Jefferson, however, did not believe that the United States could afford any hint that it might be becoming a monarchy. The idea that only a king could provide for a stable, safe, and unified government did not die easily. A British agent in America sent word to the government in London that "at this moment there is not a gentle man in the states between New Hampshire and Georgia who does not view the present government with contempt . . . and who is not desirous of changing it for a monarchy."

The debate about forms of government was as passionate in France as in the United States. "Paris is now become a furnace of politics," Jefferson wrote in May 1788. "All the world is run politically mad. Men, women, children talk nothing else."

A cold winter, a lack of bread, and frustration with the current system of government prompted riots in Paris, which led to the deaths of approximately one hundred people. Nothing was resolved by spring, and in June 1789 the French Revolution was officially under way. In the streets, citizens clashed with the army. "A more dangerous scene of war I never saw in America, than what Paris has presented for 5 days past," Jefferson wrote. The Bastille, a famous prison, was stormed and its prisoners were freed. The National Assembly was created, and its members issued the Declaration of the Rights of Man and of the Citizen. It was heavily influenced by the Declaration of Independence, and Thomas Jefferson had advised its author, his friend the Marquis de Lafayette, during its writing.

The storming of the Bastille in Paris on July 14, 1789.

THE DECLARATION OF THE RIGHTS OF MAN AND OF THE CITIZEN

Before the French Revolution, the king was advised by the Estates General, an assembly with representatives from three "estates," or groups. There was one for the noblemen and one for the church; the Third Estate represented the majority of the French people. On the eve of the revolution, the Third Estate seized power and formed the National Assembly.

One of the first actions of the National Assembly was to issue the Declaration of the Rights of Man and of the Citizen. The declaration insisted that all men were equal and that certain rights must never be taken away from citizens of France. Under the declaration, all citizens had a right to participate in making laws. Trials by jury, freedom of religion, and freedom of speech were guaranteed.

There were many similarities to Thomas Jefferson's Declaration of Independence, written thirteen years earlier.

Declaration of Independence	Declaration of the Rights of Man and of the Citizen
All men are created equal.	Men are born and remain free and equal in rights.
Among these [rights] are life, liberty and the pursuit of happiness.	These rights are Liberty, Property, Safety and Resistance to Oppression.
Governments are instituted among men, deriving their just powers from the consent of the governed.	The source of all sovereignty lies essentially in the Nation.

Lafayette hoped to prevent violence and chaos from spreading and had begged Jefferson to "break every engagement" to join him and several others from the National Assembly at a dinner where a new form of government and a new constitution for France would be debated. Jefferson, "a silent witness," as he called himself, was impressed by the sense and eloquence he heard. "So far it seemed that your revolution had got along with a steady pace," he told Lafayette, "meeting indeed with occasional difficulties and dangers, but we are not to expect to be translated [changed] from despotism [tyranny] to liberty in a feather-bed."

Lafayette was also placed in charge of the safety of King Louis XVI and Queen Marie Antoinette. Patsy Jefferson remembered standing at the window of her hotel, watching as the king and queen rode by under the protection of her father's friend. The young Frenchman, noticing Patsy at the window of her hotel, bowed to her—a mark of respect that she never forgot. All her life she kept a three-cornered hat with the blue, white, and red colors of the French flag, a memento of the early days of the revolution.

Declaration of the Rights of Man and of the Citizen, issued by the French National Assembly in 1789. This document was very similar to the Declaration of Independence.

In the streets of Paris, the king and queen were in danger from their own people. The United States, which had also revolted against a king, was now planning to elect a president. Everywhere, the ordinary order of things was being turned upside down. Jefferson's private life was no exception.

When fourteen-year-old Sally Hemings arrived in Paris with Polly Jefferson, she came to a place where the rules were different. In Virginia, she was a slave, receiving no money at all for the work that she did. In Paris, Sally was paid a small wage. (Historians are not sure exactly what her work was. She may have acted as a maid to Polly and Patsy at their school.)

While they were in Paris, Thomas Jefferson and Sally Hemings began a relationship that was to last for many years—years in which Sally remained a slave owned by Jefferson. When Jefferson prepared to return to Virginia in the fall of 1789, Sally Hemings was pregnant with their child. She told Jefferson that she did not want to go back to Virginia with him.

In Virginia, Sally had no legal way to obtain her own freedom. In Paris, she had the means of freedom in her grasp. Slaves were allowed to apply for their liberty in France. There was nothing their masters could do to prevent it.

Most Americans supported the French Revolution until the executions of Louis XVI and Marie Antoinette in 1793.

"She was just beginning to understand the French language well, and in France she was free, while if she returned to Virginia she would be re-enslaved," Sally's son Madison later said. "So she refused to go with him."

Jefferson was used to controlling all aspects of his personal and political life. Yet here was a girl nearly the same age as his oldest daughter refusing to accept his orders or do as he wished. It must have seemed unthinkable, even absurd. But she, not he, was in control.

In order to convince Sally to return to Virginia, Jefferson agreed to what Sally asked. He promised her "extraordinary privileges," Madison Hemings said. Most important, he "made a solemn pledge that her children should be freed at the age of twenty-one years."

According to her son, Sally believed Jefferson. She sailed back to Virginia with him. The child she was bearing at the time did not survive long after its birth; we do not know its sex or its name. Sally later gave birth to three more sons and one daughter—(William) Beverly, Harriet, Madison, and Eston. "Jefferson," said Madison, "was the father of all of them."

Jefferson kept his promise to Sally. All four of their children were freed from slavery when they reached twenty-one.

CHAPTER FOURTEEN

A New Post in New York

In general, I think it necessary to give as well as take in a government like ours.
—THOMAS JEFFERSON

With his daughters, Polly and Patsy, and his slaves Sally and James Hemings, Jefferson crossed the Atlantic in "fine autumn weather," reaching Virginia in November 1789. In December, he received a request from the new president, George Washington. Would Jefferson become the secretary of state, to serve as the president's chief advisor when dealing with other countries?

Jefferson hesitated. He was concerned that, in this position, he would be exposed to public criticism, something that he always found painful. "My great wish is . . . to avoid attracting notice and to keep my name out of newspapers, because I find the pain of a little censure [criticism] . . . more acute [sharp] than the pleasure of much praise," he once told a friend.

It was a familiar conflict for him: he loved attention and applause but feared failure and disapproval. It would seem easy for a man who so hated criticism to simply lead a private life, but that was something Jefferson never did. His will to serve and sacrifice was as strong as the pain he felt when others considered his service and sacrifice inadequate.

After talking with James Madison and trading more letters with Washington, Jefferson accepted. He would not return to France; instead, he would head for the nation's new capital, New York City, to work at the side of its first president. The lessons he would learn as secretary of state would guide him when he became vice president, and then president, of the United States.

Federal Hall, on New York's famous Wall Street, in 1789.

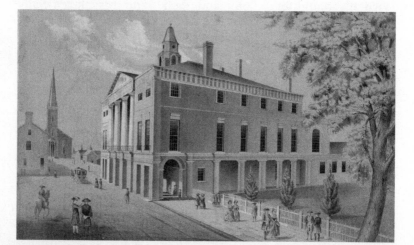

Before Jefferson left Monticello for New York, he handled the arrangements of his daughter's wedding. Shortly after her return to the United States, Patsy Jefferson married her third cousin Thomas Mann Randolph Jr. The wedding took place in February 1790.

In New York, Jefferson found a house at 57 Maiden Lane. "Mr. Jefferson is here, and adds much to the social circle," Abigail Adams wrote in April 1790. On Sunday, March 21, the secretary of state paid his first official call on the president of the United States.

Washington and Jefferson had known each other for more than twenty-five years, and the president had reason to think well of his advisor. "Nothing can excel Mr. Jefferson's abilities, virtues, pleasing temper, and everything in him that constitutes [makes up] the great statesman, zealous citizen, and amiable friend," Lafayette had told Washington two years before.

Portrait of Thomas Mann Randolph Jr., husband of Jefferson's daughter Patsy, member of Congress, and governor of Virginia.

To Jefferson, Washington had been a grand but distant figure, almost a living myth. Now he would better know the hero of the Revolutionary War. "He was incapable of fear, meeting personal dangers with the calmest unconcern," Jefferson wrote later. He found Washington a careful and deliberate man. The president thought every action through,

George Washington, whom Jefferson respected, admired, and feared—but did not love.

considered every doubt, but once he had made a decision, he went "through with his purpose, whatever obstacles opposed."

Jefferson gave Washington credit for intelligence—"His mind was great and powerful"—but not for genius. "As far as he saw, no judgment was ever sounder," Jefferson commented, but Washington's mind was "slow in operation, being little aided by invention or imagination, but sure in conclusion."

Washington's bouts of anger were daunting to Jefferson, who loved to be liked. "His temper was naturally irritable," Jefferson remarked, but usually held in check. "If however, it broke its bonds, he was most tremendous in his wrath." Washington was a man, in other words, around whom one was careful.

Now forty-seven years old, Jefferson was returning home after five years in France. At first, he felt a little out of place. He appealed to James Madison for advice often. "Be so good as to say what you think," he wrote to his friend. "I must be troublesome to you till I know better the ground on which I am placed."

He was somewhat surprised and concerned to find that he was often in the minority. Two parties had sprung up in American politics—the Federalists, who supported a strong national government, and the Republicans, who leaned toward states' rights and were concerned that power centered in a national government might mean less liberty for the people.

Jefferson had worried that the United States under its first constitution had created a national government with too little power to do its job. He now became a Republican, afraid of the opposite problem—that a democracy with a president at its head might be slipping into a monarchy. Citizens bowed to Washington; the president traveled in an enormous carriage with many horses. Would looking like a king lead to a president acting like a king? Jefferson thought it might.

Jefferson was anxious about where the national government might be headed, but he was still a practical man and politician. In the spring of 1790, he met with Alexander Hamilton, the secretary of the Treasury and a firm Federalist. Hamilton was working on a plan for the national government to take over the debts that the states had assumed during the Revolutionary War. To pay this debt, the government would need to set taxes, which would increase its power.

Hamilton and Jefferson agreed on very little. But at the moment, Hamilton needed Jefferson. His plan was dividing

Jefferson long feared that his rival Alexander Hamilton's vision of government would lead the United States back into monarchy.

the country. The Northern states (which owed the most) tended to support it; the Southern states (many of which had paid off most or all of their debts) did not.

Jefferson was uncomfortable with most of Hamilton's beliefs, but he was always a believer in compromise. He helped gather support for Hamilton's plan, and in return, Hamilton agreed to give the Southern states something they wanted—the capital of the United States. New York was already famous as the financial center of the new country. Politicians from other regions wanted the capital elsewhere. Hamilton agreed.

In 1790, the national capital was moved to Philadelphia, which would be its temporary home until the new city of Washington in the District of Columbia, along the Potomac River, could be made ready.

Hamilton and Jefferson could work together when they had to, but the rivalry between them grew tenser over the years. Their ideas of what was best for their country were very different. The disagreement was not only personal; the two men became symbols of two distinct views of how America should be governed.

The Republicans, Jefferson among them, feared monarchy or dictatorship, the power of the one over the many. Jefferson fretted over the possibility of the return of a king in some form, whether as a president whose authority had no limit or as a royal family whose power would be passed down by birth.

He was not the only one with such worries. John Adams was a Federalist himself, but even he was concerned about the possibility of powerful American families—like the Washingtons or even the Jeffersons—marrying European aristocrats. He wrote to Jefferson:

> *If the Duke of Angouleme, or Burgundy, or especially the Dauphin [the prince of France] should demand one of your beautiful and most amiable daughters in marriage, all America from Georgia to New Hampshire would find their vanity and pride so agreeably flattered by it that all their sage maxims [wise ideas] would give way; and even our sober New England Republicans would keep a day*

French queen Marie Antoinette and her children in 1787.

of thanksgiving for it, in their hearts. If General Washington had a daughter, I firmly believe, she would be demanded in marriage by one of the royal families of France or England, perhaps by both, or if he had a son he would be invited to come a courting to Europe.

Anxieties about the return of a monarchy were mingled with fears about England. Jefferson was always on the watch for hints that Great Britain meant to try to take control of its former colony once again. Such hints were there to be found. An American lawyer wrote to Jefferson from England, warning him that the king was still angry with the Americans and that "if we could be smitten without the hazard of a general war," the British would not hesitate to attack.

It is easiest to understand Thomas Jefferson's passion for liberty and his championship of democracy by seeing him as a man who believed there were forces everywhere—visible and invisible, inside and outside his country—trying to deny the people their rights and to restore the rule of nobles and kings.

Where Jefferson regarded Great Britain with suspicion, Hamilton, the Federalist, saw the country as America's natural ally. "I have always preferred a connection with you, to that of any other country," Hamilton once told a British agent, hoping his feelings would be shared with the British government. *"We think in English,* and have a similarity of prejudices and predilections [preferences]."

Hamilton believed that the best way for the United States to achieve long-lasting stability would be for its government to resemble that of Great Britain as much as possible. If some of the British system's faults could be corrected, he once said, "it would be the most perfect constitution of government ever devised by man." He was doubtful about regular elections and widespread voting rights, worrying that they could lead to chaos. In a speech to the Constitutional Convention, he had argued that America would be better off with a king.

Over time, Jefferson came to see Hamilton as his worst fear come true: a powerful man, trusted by the president, who might be willing to sacrifice American liberties for the sake of a powerful, central authority. And Hamilton came to see Jefferson as a man who might be willing to throw away everything the Americans had built by giving way to the kind of turmoil that was slowly building in France as the revolution there continued.

In later years, when his feelings had calmed, Jefferson bought a bust of Alexander Hamilton. He placed the statue in the entrance hall of Monticello, opposite one of himself. "Opposed in death as in life," Jefferson remarked once about the two statues.

The Magna Carta, a thirteenth-century document outlining English common law. It states that the law is above everyone—even the king.

The French Revolution

In the beginning, support for the French Revolution was widespread among Americans. "We were all strongly attached to France—scarcely any man more than myself," remembered John Marshall, Jefferson's cousin and the chief justice of the United States Supreme Court. "I sincerely believed human liberty to depend in a great measure on the success of the French Revolution."

From the autumn of 1792 onward, however, the revolution became bloodier and bloodier. King Louis XVI and Queen Marie Antoinette were executed in 1793, and 1794 saw the beginning of the Reign of Terror, when the revolutionaries seemed willing to bring to the guillotine anyone they suspected of being against their cause. The Marquis de Lafayette, Jefferson's friend and a hero of the American Revolution, was forced to flee the country. France entered into war with many European countries, including England and Spain.

Opinions in America became divided. Men like Alexander Hamilton saw the violence of the revolution as proof of the need for a strong government to keep chaos at bay. Thomas Jefferson lost friends to the guillotine and mourned for them. But his support for the French Revolution did not waver. "In the struggle which was necessary, many guilty persons fell without the forms of trial, and with them some innocent," he wrote. "These I deplore [regret] as much as anyone, and shall deplore some of them to the day of my death. But I deplore them as I should have done had they fallen in battle.... The liberty of the whole earth was depending on the issue of the contest [the result of the war], and was ever such a prize won with so little innocent blood?"

Illustration of Louis XVI being led to the guillotine for his execution in 1793.

The conflict between the two men helped to shape the early years of American democracy, but they were colleagues as well as rivals, working together to build a government and a nation.

Bust of Alexander Hamilton by Giuseppe Ceracchi.

Bust of Thomas Jefferson by Jean-Antoine Houdon.

CHAPTER FIFTEEN
In Wait at Monticello

I live on my horse from an early breakfast to a late dinner, and very often after that till dark.
—THOMAS JEFFERSON

Jefferson and Hamilton were both members of the president's cabinet, or his circle of official advisors, and were at odds every day. Each tried hard to sway George Washington to his own way of thinking, while Washington tried to hear both out and to find a balance in the midst of their sharp disagreements. "For I will frankly and solemnly declare that I believe the views of both of you are pure, and well-meant," he wrote to Jefferson in 1792.

In this painting, Jefferson and Hamilton consult with President Washington. Though Jefferson and Hamilton often disagreed, both were patriots fighting for the greater good of the country.

Jefferson could not accept this view, and he did not hesitate to warn Washington about the dangers of Hamilton and the Federalists. Their goal, he told the president, was "to prepare the way for a change from the present republican form of government to that of a monarchy."

Jefferson sometimes suspected even the president himself of thinking like a king. Once, when he grew impatient with Congress, Washington complained that "he did not like throwing too much into democratic hands" and suggested that if Congress "would not do what the Constitution called on them to do, the government would be at an end, and must *then assume another form.*"

For Jefferson, the images of monarchy swirled. The grand promises and vision of the American Revolution—the ones that Jefferson himself had put into words—seemed to be growing fainter in the clatter of a city that, to Jefferson, was beginning to feel more like a king's court than the capital of a republic.

Jefferson feared not only that Americans would turn to a king but that the country might split apart. The Southern states, which tended to be more Republican than those in the Northeast, might break away. Only one thing held them together at the moment: George Washington. "The confidence of the whole union is centered in you. . . . North and South will hang together, if they have you to hang on," he told the president.

Washington felt himself to be growing old and was worried that seeking another term as president could make him look greedy for public power. But he was persuaded to continue as president for a second term, and he wanted Jefferson to stay on as well. Would Jefferson consider returning to France to represent American interests there? Jefferson politely refused.

Washington was not pleased. Jefferson "had pressed" the president to "a continuance in public service and [now] refused to do the same." Diplomatically, Jefferson insisted that the two cases were different. There was only one George Washington; no one else could keep the country unified.

But "a thousand others could supply my place," Jefferson said. Washington gave in.

To defy George Washington was not an easy thing, but Jefferson did it. It was a moment that clearly showed Jefferson's political skill. He was a man who got his way quietly but unmistakably, without bluster, his words pleasant but his will firm.

Washington entered another term as president, and Jefferson stayed on for a time as secretary of state. But the conflicts with Hamilton and the Federalists continued. Jefferson longed to hear news of home in the midst of arguments and anxieties. "From Monticello you have everything to write about which I have any care," he told his family. "How do my young chestnut trees? How comes on your garden? How fare the fruit blossoms etc."

After a quarter of a century spent serving in his country's government, in revolution, in war, and in a fragile peace, Jefferson was tired. "Worn out with labors from morning till night and day to day," he complained, he was "giving everything I love, in exchange for everything I hate." At the end of 1793, Jefferson offered Washington his resignation. The president took it "with sincere regret."

Others were less generous. The long friendship between John Adams and Thomas Jefferson had been damaged. Adams was a Federalist, Jefferson a Republican, and their political disagreements had become personal. Adams wrote angrily,

In 1770, Jefferson drew these plans for slave quarters at Monticello, later called Mulberry Row.

"Jefferson went off yesterday, and a good riddance to bad ware. He has talents I know, and integrity I believe; but his mind is now poisoned with passion, prejudice, and faction."

Back in Virginia, Jefferson threw himself into making his home exactly what he wanted it to be. He tore down the original house at Monticello and began work on a larger, grander one. "Architecture is my delight," he said, "and putting up and pulling down one of my favorite amusements." As well as doubling the size of his house, Jefferson added new slave quarters, a smokehouse, a dairy, a blacksmith's shop, a carpenter's shop, and a washhouse. In April 1794, he started a nailery, where enslaved boys made as many as ten thousand nails a day.

Monticello was its own world. "Every article is made on his farm," a French visitor remarked. "His negroes are cabinet-makers, carpenters, masons, bricklayers, smiths, etc. The children he employs in a nail-factory. . . . The young and old negresses spin for the clothing of the rest."

Jefferson suffered from rheumatism, or pain in the joints, but took much pleasure in being home once more. He hunted deer, rabbit, and partridge, and he fished (he had a favorite spot "below the old dam" on the Rivanna River). It was a great source of joy to him to be near his family again. He wrote of his grandson Thomas Jefferson Randolph: "He has not worn his shoes an hour this winter. If put on him, he takes them off immediately and uses one to carry his nuts etc. in. Within these two days we have put both him and Ann [his sister] into moccasins, which being made of soft leather, fitting well and lacing up, they have never been able to take them off."

A Moment on Mulberry Row by Nathaniel Gibbs depicts the life of slaves on Jefferson's estate.

Jefferson spoke and wrote as though he would not stir from Monticello again. "My private business can never call me elsewhere, and certainly politics will not," he insisted.

But his time at home lasted only about two years. He stayed in touch with all that was happening in Philadelphia by letter, writing to John Adams about the latest threat of war with Great Britain. England, in the midst of a war with France, was interfering with American ships. Americans also worried that the British were supporting the Barbary pirates and encouraging hostile Native American tribes on the American frontier.

Jefferson and his friends were concerned about war with Great Britain but equally concerned about a Federalist proposal to create a new army of fifteen thousand men. Was the purpose of this army to defend the United States from Great Britain, or was it to establish the president as a dictator? "A change so extraordinary must have a serious object [point] in view," James Monroe wrote to Jefferson.

Jefferson worried, also, about Washington's anger toward groups called Democratic-Republican societies. These groups, supporters of the Republican Party, became connected in Washington's mind with the Whiskey Rebellion, an outburst of violence in Pennsylvania over taxes on liquor. There was no direct connection, but to the president, both the violence and the outspoken groups who opposed his government were threats of disorder, chaos, and disaster.

"The attempt which has been made to restrain the liberty of our citizens meeting together, interchanging sentiments on what subjects they please, and stating these sentiments in the public papers, has come upon us, a full century earlier than I expected," Jefferson wrote. He dismissed the Whiskey Rebellion and instead concentrated on what he saw as the attempts of his political enemies to cut off free speech.

Jefferson had found rest and refuge at home. What he may not have realized was how closely he remained connected to politics. The life of the nation was as much a part of his

A painting of President Washington and his troops marching to suppress the Whiskey Rebellion.

own life as science or music or Monticello. He could no more ignore what was happening in the wider world than he could choose to stop being interested in science or books. Politics was not only what Thomas Jefferson practiced. It was part of who he was, even if he himself sometimes failed to see it.

Others saw it clearly.

John Jay, with the help of Alexander Hamilton, had negotiated a treaty with London to end the threat of war. Jefferson and the Republicans despised the treaty, believing it was much too generous to England. Even George Washington's support could not keep the Jay Treaty from being widely hated.

The treaty pushed Jefferson into considering a new idea. Ever since the new constitution, there was one position in the United States government that had more power than any other: the presidency. Suppose the president were a Republican? Suppose that Republican were Jefferson?

A lawmaker from Tennessee put the matter plainly in a letter to Jefferson. He wrote to inform him that "the people of this State, of every

John Jay, one of the Founding Fathers, was very involved in foreign policy and served as the chief justice of the United States Supreme Court. While governor of New York, he refused Alexander Hamilton's request to alter election laws, which could have denied Jefferson the presidency in 1800.

description, express a wish that you should be the next President of the United States."

Jefferson's reply was not completely clear. "I have not the arrogance to say I would refuse the honorable office you mention to me," he wrote back. "But I can say with truth that I would rather be thought worthy of it than to be appointed to it." Always sensitive to criticism, Jefferson pointed out that "well I know that no man will ever bring out of that office the reputation which carries him into it."

CHAPTER SIXTEEN

To the Vice Presidency

There is a debt of service due from every man to his country.
—THOMAS JEFFERSON

The publication of George Washington's farewell speech on Monday, September 19, 1796, set off America's first race for the presidency. No one had run against George Washington. That was not going to be the case for the country's next president. Jefferson wanted the job, and so did John Adams. Alexander Hamilton did not want Jefferson or Adams, and he supported Thomas Pinckney from South Carolina.

In the presidential campaigns of the 1700s, candidates did not campaign, give speeches, or travel the country, seeking votes. They let it be known, often by telling friends and allies, that they would be willing to be elected. Electors then cast votes for the president. In five states, the electors were chosen by the voters; in eleven others, the electors were chosen by the lawmakers (who had been elected by the voters). The candidate with the most electoral votes became president; the second-place finisher, vice president.

When it came to presidential elections, however, one thing was the same as today: they were full of attacks and counterattacks. Ten days after Washington's farewell address was published, Jefferson's enemies struck hard.

A Federalist lawyer, a supporter of John Adams, criticized Jefferson, calling him a coward for fleeing the invading British army when he was governor of Virginia. Such a man was too weak to be president, the Adams supporters said, "for no one can know how soon or from whence a storm comes." Jefferson's allies hit back, calling Adams a "monarchist," a man devoted to the idea of inherited power.

Jefferson waited at Monticello to hear the results of the election. A late-autumn spell of cold weather froze the ink in the inkwell on his desk. Thinking about what the next leader of the country would have to do, Jefferson wondered whether it would actually be better to come in second in the race, winning the vice presidency. "I do sincerely wish to be the second on the vote rather than the first," he wrote. If he and Adams ended up with a tied vote, he thought Adams should become the president. "He has always been my senior . . . and the expression of the public will being equal, this circumstance ought to give him the preference."

On Wednesday, February 8, 1797, the votes of the electors were tallied. John Adams won, barely, with seventy-one votes to Jefferson's sixty-eight. (Pinckney came in third, with fifty-nine.) The president would be a Federalist; the vice president, a Republican. The two disagreed on politics, had watched as their supporters fought viciously during the campaign, and were now supposed to work together to lead the country.

Jefferson reached Philadelphia on Thursday, March 2, 1797. Without delay, he visited Adams, who returned the courtesy by calling on Jefferson the next morning. The two had much to talk about.

They spoke of France. Adams had considered sending Jefferson on a diplomatic mission to Paris. On second thought, he had decided that it would be irresponsible to ship the vice president out of the country. What did Jefferson think of sending James Madison instead? Jefferson was doubtful; he thought that Madison would refuse. Adams was determined. "He said that if Mr. Madison should refuse, he would still appoint him and leave the responsibility to him," Jefferson remembered.

Jefferson and Adams were sworn in on March 4, 1797. Once again, Jefferson told his friends that he was happy to have the vice presidency. "The second office of this government is honorable and easy," he said. "The first is but a splendid misery."

Two days after they began their new jobs, Adams and Jefferson had dinner with George Washington. They left the table together, and as they walked home, they discussed the question of France once more.

Adams had decided not to send James Madison on the mission after all. The new president had spent time with his advisors that day, and several of them objected to the idea of sending a Republican like Madison to France. Jefferson remembered the new president "going on with excuses which evidently embarrassed him" before they parted ways. "And he never after that said one word to me on the subject," Jefferson finished, "or ever consulted me as to any measures of government."

John Adams governed amid stress and strain. For a time, he fought to keep the peace (what there was of it) as tensions grew between the United States and France, its first and most important ally. The French, in the midst of a war with England, resented the fact that American ships were beginning to trade with Great Britain. French ships seized American ones on the seas in what Adams called "the half-war with France." At last, the president warned his country that all-out war might be coming.

The constant threat of violence created a feeling of crisis at every moment and made it nearly impossible for Federalists and Republicans to cooperate. Each party was convinced that the other's policies could quickly lead to disaster. One Republican congressman even spat in the face of a Federalist congressman, and the two brawled with a cane and fireplace tongs on the floor of the House of Representatives.

Etching of a fight between Representatives Matthew Lyon and Roger Griswold on the House floor. Griswold attacked Lyon with a cane, and Lyon grabbed a pair of fireplace tongs to defend himself.

As Adams's vice president, Thomas Jefferson spent most of his time presiding over the Senate and quietly building the Republican opposition to the Federalist government. He was the champion of individual rights against what he saw as the president's attempts to curb or destroy those rights in the name of unity against a powerful enemy.

The main cause of concern for Jefferson and the Republicans was four laws known as the Alien and Sedition Acts. These laws were designed to give the president extraordinary powers, powers that Jefferson and his friends believed belonged to the people. The president was allowed to deport, or send out of the country, foreigners whom he considered dangerous. It was forbidden to "write, print, utter, or publish . . . any false, scandalous, and malicious writing or writings against the government of the United States." Writers could be sent to prison for criticizing the government or the president; newspaper publishers could be imprisoned for printing their articles or letters.

Republican newspaper editors were arrested and tried for publishing articles that the Adams government disapproved of. James Thomson Callender, a Republican whom Jefferson had supported financially, was sent to prison for publishing a little book with a high-minded title—*The Prospect Before Us*. It was an open attack on John Adams. "As president, he has never opened his lips, or lifted his pen, without threatening and scolding," Callender wrote. "The grand object of his administration has been . . . to destroy every man who differs from his opinions."

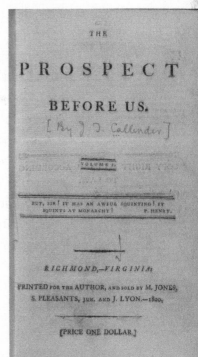

In *The Prospect Before Us,* James Thomson Callender openly attacked President John Adams and his administration.

Jefferson had told Callender that his book "cannot fail to produce the best effect." The effect it produced was to send Callender to prison and to saddle him with a fine of two hundred dollars. The Republican congressman Matthew Lyon was also tried and sentenced to four months in jail and a fine of one thousand dollars for writing a letter to the *Vermont Journal* against the sedition law.

Jefferson and the Republicans decided that they were no longer expecting the end of American liberty—that end was here. "If this goes down, we shall immediately see attempted another act of Congress declaring that the President shall continue in office during life," Jefferson declared. And that would be the death of what Jefferson's generation had fought for.

Adams and the Federalists, on the other hand, believed they were limiting some of the problems that liberty brought with it, but only in order to defend liberty itself. The danger of war was real, and war called for extraordinary measures.

Jefferson could not have disagreed more. He encouraged Republicans to run for Congress and secretly drafted a resolution protesting the Alien and Sedition Acts for the state legislature in Kentucky to send to the president. (James Madison did the same for Virginia.) The vice president of the United States was actually at work on an official rebuke for one of the American states to send to the president.

During the bitter conflict of his years as vice president, Thomas Jefferson began to have a different reaction to the criticism he faced. "I have been for some time used as the property of the newspapers, a fair mark for every man's dirt," he grumbled. But that he saw this as simply something to be endured as a part of political life was a more mature view and a sign that Jefferson could grow and learn. He did not have to like the public attacks, but he knew he had to put up with them if he wanted a life in politics.

Jefferson's political style continued to be smooth rather than rough, polite rather than challenging. "No one can know Mr. Jefferson and be his *personal* enemy," said the Supreme Court justice who had presided over Matthew Lyon's trial.

Jefferson was a warrior for the causes in which he believed, but he waged his battles carefully. He used friends and allies to write and publish, sending out the messages he thought the public needed to hear. Face to face, he was ever gracious and courteous. Part of this was his Virginia upbringing, which taught that good manners were vital. And part was a calculated decision, based on his experience, that direct conflict did little good.

In a long, thoughtful letter to a grandson, Jefferson set his thoughts about human relationships into words. "A determination never to do what is wrong, prudence, and good humor," he advised, were what was needed to obtain the good opinion of the world. Then he added more rules for his grandson to remember:

> *I must not omit the important one of never entering into a dispute or argument with another. I never yet saw an instance of one of two disputants [opponents] convincing the other by argument. I have seen many, of their getting warm [angry], becoming rude, and shooting one another. . . . It was one of the rules which above all others made Doctr. Franklin the most amiable of men in society, never to contradict anybody.*

While his country was more or less at war with France, and its two political parties were nearly at war with each other, much was also happening in Jefferson's personal life. Patsy Randolph had three children, giving Jefferson three grandchildren. Polly married John Wayles Eppes, a cousin, in 1797. Sally Hemings gave birth to a son (William Beverly, called Beverly) in 1798; in that same year, her two-year-old daughter, Harriet, died. A second daughter, who was not to live long, was born in December of the next year. Jefferson had fathered all three children.

CHAPTER SEVENTEEN

A Desperate State of Affairs

It is extremely uncertain on whom the choice will fall.
—JOHN MARSHALL

As the eighteenth century ended, a new presidential election would be held. Jefferson was determined to seek the top office again, and so was John Adams. So much seemed at stake. Republicans suspected that Adams would make himself into a king. To Federalists, Jefferson, a longtime supporter of religious freedom, was a dangerous infidel (one who does not believe in the Christian God) or even an atheist (one who does not believe in any god at all).

George Washington died in 1799. Jefferson chose to stay at Monticello rather than attend any of the many ceremonies celebrating Washington's life. He had admired Washington's gifts in the art of leadership, but he could not help seeing that Washington had become a symbol for the Federalists. And Jefferson believed the Federalists were attacking American liberty.

Alexander Hamilton, not Thomas Jefferson, felt himself to be Washington's true heir. "Perhaps no man in this community has equal cause with myself to deplore the loss,"

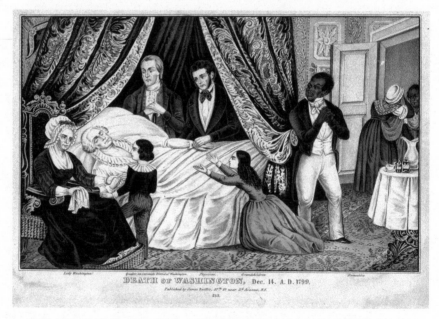

Death of Washington by James Baillie depicts George Washington on his deathbed at his Mount Vernon estate in 1799.

Hamilton said of Washington's death. "I have been very much indebted to the kindness of the General." Hamilton hated the idea of Jefferson as president and did his best to make sure his own state, New York, would not cast its votes for his political enemy. He asked the state's governor, John Jay, to change the election laws to make sure Jefferson would not be chosen. "In times like this in which we live," Hamilton told the governor, "it will not do to be overscrupulous." The goal, Hamilton insisted, was to "prevent an *atheist* in religion and a *fanatic* in politics" from becoming president.

John Jay refused to change the laws. It was an action, he wrote to Hamilton, "which I think it would not become me to adopt." New York cast its electoral votes for Jefferson.

On the day he heard the news of the New York results, Jefferson met with Adams. "Well, I understand that you are to beat me in this contest," Adams told Jefferson, "and I will only say that I will be as faithful a subject as any you will have."

"Mr. Adams, this is no personal contest between you and me," Jefferson, always courteous, replied.

Slowly but steadily in the fall of 1800, results from the states reached Jefferson at Monticello. Republicans were winning where they needed to win. On Friday, December 12, Jefferson wrote that "I believe we may consider the election as now decided." But the possibility of a tie between Thomas Jefferson and another Republican candidate, Aaron Burr, was

Aaron Burr was a daunting political force. After he tied Jefferson in the 1800 presidential election, Jefferson never trusted him again.

worrisome. A tie was supposed to be decided by a vote in the House of Representatives, but Jefferson feared that the Federalists there would try to install a different president, perhaps the new chief justice, John Marshall.

By the last Sunday in December, all the votes were in—and Jefferson's fears were realized. It was a tie.

Jefferson tried to stay calm. It was not easy. "The election," he wrote to a son-in-law, "is still problematical."

That was putting it mildly. Jefferson's enemies were worried that his presidency would be a disaster. "There would be really cause to fear that the government would not survive the course of moral and political experiments to which it would be subjected in the hands of Mr. Jefferson," one Federalist congressman fretted.

Republicans, on the other hand, were sure that the fate of democracy was at stake. "What will be the plans of the Federalists? Will they usurp the Presidential powers? . . . I see some danger in the fate of the election," one wrote. Some of Jefferson's supporters considered arming themselves and marching on the capital. The governor of Pennsylvania made plans for calling out the militia if anyone but Jefferson or Burr was appointed president by Congress.

Jefferson was worried enough by talk of installing a kind

of temporary president that he went to see John Adams and asked him to veto any such measure. Hearing Jefferson's business, Adams flew into a temper. "He grew warm in an instant," Jefferson recalled, and answered his vice president with an intensity "he had not used towards me before."

"Sir," Adams said to Jefferson, "the event [outcome] of the election is in your own hands." He insisted that if Jefferson would only agree to follow certain Federalist policies, he would be made president at once. The government, Adams said, would "instantly be put in your hands."

Jefferson did not like the sound of this. "I will not come into the government by capitulation," he said. "I will not enter on it but in perfect freedom to follow the dictates of my own judgment."

"Then things must take their course," Adams answered, and the conversation ended.

It was a bitter, uncomfortable moment, "the first time in our lives we had ever parted with anything like dissatisfaction," Jefferson recalled.

While the election remained undecided, John Adams and the Federalists took advantage of their last moments in power. They changed the number of Supreme Court justices from six to five, making it very unlikely that the next president would be able to appoint a justice to the highest court in the country. They created new courts and appointed Federalist judges to them. Adams also appointed John Marshall, Jefferson's

John Marshall was appointed as chief justice just before Jefferson took office as president. He defended Federalist interests and helped establish the principle of judicial review.

cousin and a lifelong foe of his, as the chief justice of the Supreme Court. The appointment was for life. Jefferson, if he became president, would not be able to change it.

The tension exhausted Jefferson. "I long to be in the midst of the children, and have more pleasure in their little follies than in the wisdom of the wise," he wrote to Patsy. "Here too there is such a mixture of the bad passions of the heart that one feels themselves in an enemy's country."

The House of Representatives planned to meet on Wednesday, February 11, 1801, to choose a president. Even Alexander Hamilton seemed willing to throw his support to Jefferson as the best of two bad choices. "Jefferson is to be preferred" over Aaron Burr, he said. "He is by far not so dangerous a man; and he has pretensions to character."

The voting went on for days. The weather was terrible. Lawmakers slept on makeshift mattresses on the floor, and one politician was carried through the snow on a stretcher to the House; his wife guided his hand to help him make a choice.

Finally, at one p.m. on Tuesday, February 17, 1801, the vote was decided. Jefferson had won. John Adams would leave the presidency, and Thomas Jefferson would take over the office.

A banner commemorating Jefferson's 1800 presidential victory.

Despite all the strain of recent years, Jefferson and the Adamses had usually managed to maintain quietly civil relations. Before Abigail Adams left Washington, she received Thomas Jefferson for tea. As Abigail told it, Jefferson "made me a visit . . . in order to take leave and wish me a good journey. It was more than I expected."

They had been through so much with one another. Politics had brought them together, and politics had now driven them apart. And yet they still found it in themselves to treat one another with outward courtesy and grace.

Jefferson was delighted by the outcome of the election but serious about the work that lay ahead. The duty of the president, as he saw it, was to "unite in himself the confidence of the whole people . . . and point them in a single direction," as if they made up "but one body and one mind."

And he knew how hard that would be. "I sincerely thank you for your congratulations on my election, but this is only the first verse of the chapter," he wrote a friend. "What the last may be nobody can tell."

CHAPTER EIGHTEEN

The New Order of Things Begins

It must be admitted you have much trouble and difficulty to encounter.
—JAMES MONROE

As noon approached on Wednesday, March 4, 1801, Thomas Jefferson prepared to make the short walk from his boarding-house to the Capitol. Riflemen from Alexandria, Virginia, formed a small parade, along with a company of militia officers and a group of congressmen. As he approached the

Capitol, the militiamen drew their swords and parted to allow the new president through.

About a thousand people were waiting for Jefferson in the Senate. John Marshall, the chief justice, heard Jefferson recite the oath of office. In his weak voice, which few in the room could hear clearly, Jefferson then gave the first speech of his presidency.

It was one of the most important speeches in American history, calling for both freedom and tolerance.

All . . . will bear in mind this sacred principle, that though the will of the majority is in all cases to prevail, that will to be rightful must be reasonable; that the minority possess their equal rights, which equal law must protect. . . . Let us then, fellow-citizens, unite with one heart and one mind. . . . We are all Republicans, we are all Federalists. . . . I repair, then, fellow-citizens, to the post you have assigned me. . . . I shall often go wrong through defect of judgment. When right, I shall often be thought wrong. . . . I ask your indulgence for my own errors, which will never be intentional, and your support against the errors of others.

Thomas Jefferson took the presidential oath of office in 1801, administered by Chief Justice John Marshall.

The address was a political masterpiece. It calmed the fears of many Federalists that Jefferson was a radical who would throw away all the gains the United States had made under its second constitution. Alexander Hamilton thought the speech was "a pledge to the community, that the new president will not lend himself to dangerous innovations." A friend of Jefferson's noted with admiration that "old friends who had been separated by party names . . . shook hands with each other, immediately after reading [the speech], and discovered, for the first time, that they had differed in *opinion* only, about the best means of promoting the interests of their common country."

John Adams, the previous president, had already left Washington, grieving over the recent death of his son. But even in his sorrow, he found time to write a gracious note to Jefferson. "I sincerely wish you may never experience anything in any degree resembling" his own grief, he wrote, and added, "This part of the Union is in a state of perfect tranquility and I see nothing to obscure your prospect of a quiet and prosperous administration, which I heartily wish you."

THE OATH OF OFFICE

All presidents since George Washington have taken the oath of office, a solemn promise to fulfill the duties of the president. The president says:

I do solemnly swear [or affirm] that I will faithfully execute the Office of President of the United States, and will to the best of my ability preserve, protect and defend the Constitution of the United States.

Many presidents have added, "So help me, God."

Jefferson privately admitted to worry and anxiety as he took up his duties as president. "I feel a great load of public favor and of public expectations," he wrote the day after he took office. "More confidence is placed in me than my qualifications merit, and I dread the disappointment of my friends."

But his fears did not keep him from using his new powers. Throughout his years as president, Jefferson maintained or expanded the authority of the presidential office. The Republicans may have spoken powerfully about making sure the government's power was limited, but now that power was in his own hands, Jefferson was determined to use it for what he saw as the country's good.

He brought down the national debt and cut taxes and spending. Since he governed in a time of peace (the "half-war" with France ended before he took office), he reduced spending on the military.

Open political warfare was not for him. He preferred to influence the course of events quietly, without drama. But he understood that the country was open to—even eager for—a government that seemed less controlling and less overbearing than the one Washington and Adams had created.

Jefferson had long cared about two things: American liberty and American strength. During his eight years as president, he gathered all the power he required to make America more like what he thought it should be.

Writing to a friend, Jefferson allowed his imagination to take flight. "This whole chapter in the history of man is new. The great extent of our republic is new," he exclaimed. But he was practical as well and understood that he would not be able to accomplish everything he might dream of. "No more good must be attempted than the nation can bear," he wrote.

A friend hoped that *"Politics* will not make you forget what is due to *science."* In fact, Jefferson saw them as connected. Personal liberty created a sense of free inquiry. A free man would have a free mind, free to roam and to grow and to create and to come up with new ideas. This was Jefferson's ideal republic—and he was committed to making it real.

He moved into the President's House. For his office, he took a room in the southwest corner of the first floor, overlooking the Potomac River. He kept geraniums in the window and mockingbirds at hand. He'd had mockingbirds as pets since the 1770s, and he cherished the birds for their music. Sometimes he opened their cages to allow them to flit about his office. One bird, called Dick, would perch on his shoulder or nibble food from his lips, and it would hop up the stairs after him when he went to his bedroom to rest.

At Monticello, Jefferson was used to transforming his surroundings to suit his taste, and he did the same at the President's House. He ordered a wooden latrine on the lawn to

THE PRESIDENT'S HOUSE

In 1792, a public competition was held to decide on the design for a house where the president could live. Thomas Jefferson submitted a design anonymously, signing it with the initials "A.Z." His was not chosen. The winner was an Irish American named James Hoban, with his design for an elegant mansion with three floors and more than a hundred rooms.

John Adams was the first president to live in the President's House, moving in on November 1, 1800, even though the building was not entirely finished. On his second night there, he wrote a letter to his wife, Abigail, saying, "May none but Honest and Wise Men ever rule under this Roof."

The building was first whitewashed and later painted white. It was officially called the President's House but was nicknamed the White House early on. In 1901, President Theodore Roosevelt made the nickname official.

Jefferson's design for the President's House, submitted for consideration in 1792.

The President's House during James Madison's presidency.

155

be torn down and had the parts for indoor toilets ("water closets . . . of superior construction") sent from Philadelphia. He decided which pieces of furniture should stay and which should go. He made sure bells were hung so that he could summon his servants whenever he needed them. Neither Patsy nor Polly came to live with him in Washington, and there is no record that Sally Hemings ever made a visit to the President's House.

From the moment he took the oath of office, Jefferson set himself against the Federalist traditions of Washington and Adams. He did not wear a ceremonial sword to his swearing-in, as both previous presidents had done. He soon sold President Adams's coaches and silver harnesses, a symbolic strike against the kind of finery that made the president look like a king.

His actions were more than symbolic. He pardoned some of the printers who had been sent to prison for publishing writing that criticized the government. The case of his old ally James Thomson Callender, who had written *The Prospect Before Us,* was the most personal for him. Callender's pardon was issued on March 16, 1801.

Callender wanted more than his freedom; he also wanted Jefferson to return

In April 1789, George Washington gave the first inaugural address to a session of Congress in Federal Hall, setting a precedent that has been followed by every president since.

the two hundred dollars that he had been fined or to give him a job, perhaps as postmaster of Richmond. This Jefferson refused to do. "I now begin to know what ingratitude is," Callender complained. Callender had been a powerful ally earlier, during the sharpest conflicts between John Adams and Thomas Jefferson. But perhaps Jefferson now found his fiery political attacks unnecessary—or even a little embarrassing.

In the end, Jefferson sent his secretary, Meriwether Lewis, to offer Callender fifty dollars. But the gesture was too late. Callender sent Jefferson a message back, warning him that "he was in possession of things which he could and would use" and that he had taken the fifty dollars "as hush money."

Angry and hurt, Callender waited for the right time to take his revenge.

⟫ ⟪

The members of Jefferson's cabinet, his closest advisors, represented all the major regions of the country. James Madison (from Virginia) was his secretary of state, in charge of relations with foreign countries. Albert Gallatin (from Pennsylvania) became head of the Treasury Department. Henry Dearborn (from Massachusetts) became secretary of war. Levi Lincoln (from Massachusetts) was to be attorney general. Robert Smith (from Maryland) became secretary of the navy.

One tradition set by George Washington that Jefferson planned to keep was to be in on every detail, and he sent his cabinet a note reminding them that as president, Washington had seen nearly all letters of business sent out by members of the cabinet. "By this means," Jefferson wrote, the president "was always in accurate possession of all facts."

This was how Jefferson wanted things, too. He wanted to know everything. He *had* to know everything.

By mid-November 1801, Jefferson had settled into a routine, or what he called "a steady and uniform course." He worked from ten to thirteen hours a day at his writing table and greeted visitors from early morning until midday. That gave him, he figured, "4 hours for riding, dining, and a little unbending." At noon he tried to leave the President's House for a ride or a walk before returning to be "engaged with company until candle-light." It was only on a rare night that he spent time on the "mechanics, mathematics, philosophy, etc." that he loved.

Jefferson governed personally. He knew no other way. He had watched his cousin Peyton Randolph lead the House of Burgesses in Williamsburg, gathering lawmakers at his own house to meet and talk. Jefferson did the same in Washington, since he knew that the personal attention of the president meant the world to politicians and ordinary people alike.

He believed that lawmakers and the president should be in constant conversation. He had to be able to trust the members of Congress with his thoughts, sharing insights and opinions. This created a sense that they were all on one side, working together. Making speeches at other politicians was not the best way to earn their loyalty or their help. Inviting them to dinner was much more effective.

The strategy worked. Republicans admitted that "the president's dinners had silenced them" when they were planning to vote against something Jefferson wanted.

Jefferson's red silk under-waistcoat, worn over a shirt and underneath an outer-waistcoat.

President Washington had made sure to appear formal and dignified at all times. President Jefferson greeted callers as though he had just come in from a ride. (Sometimes he had.) He wore old frock coats, velveteen breeches, knitted stockings, and ancient slippers. "Mr. Jefferson has put aside all showing off; he greets guests in slovenly [sloppy] clothes and without the least formality," a visitor wrote. "He leaves every day on foot or on horseback . . . and without even being accompanied by a servant."

A British diplomat was also surprised by Jefferson's casual manner. "The door opened suddenly" as the man approached the President's House, and there was the president himself. "He thrust out his hand to me as he does to everybody, and desired me to sit down," the guest remembered. "He is dressed and looks extremely like a very plain farmer, and wears his slippers down at his heels."

Jefferson knew what he was doing. He was no country yokel; he was, rather, who he was, with no desire to impress others with fancy clothes or formality. "You know Virginians have some pride" in dressing simply, another visitor wrote after meeting the president. They "are willing to rest their claims to attention upon their force of mind" and their smooth manners.

Jefferson knew exactly what impression he wanted his visitors to carry away with them. When a European scientist visited the President's House, he noticed a Federalist newspaper, which strongly criticized the Republicans, lying about. "Why are these libels allowed?" the visitor asked the president. Why didn't Jefferson drive the newspaper out of business or have "its editor at least, fined and imprisoned"?

"Put that paper in your pocket," Jefferson told his caller. "And should you hear the reality of our liberty, the freedom of our press, questioned, show this paper, and tell where you found it."

❧ ❧

Jefferson's confidence in himself and in his leadership was clear. He believed that the results of the 1800 election meant the people wanted change, and he was determined to create it. He exercised his power quietly, but he did exercise it, keeping himself in command of the presidency and making his wishes known to Congress, where the laws were made. Jefferson tended to get his way, as he had for so long, by smoothly but firmly bending the world to his will as much as he could.

Republican success in the elections of 1800 had given Jefferson a Congress that was unlikely to oppose him. He used his power with lawmakers, convincing Congress to end all national taxes, establish the U.S. Military Academy at West Point, and (perhaps most important) abolish the new courts and new judges that John Adams had created in his last days as president.

Jefferson encouraged lawmakers to allow the states to take the lead when it came to politics at home. When dealing with other nations, however, Jefferson was not afraid to seize the lead himself. He sent a squadron of ships to the Barbary States to protect American ships from piracy, and he made sure the commander had full authority to act "by sinking, burning, or destroying their ships and vessels wherever you

An oil painting of a sea battle with Barbary pirates.

shall find them" if any of those states declared war. He asked Congress for approval of his action—*after* he had already taken it. Congress approved.

Alexander Hamilton, among others, was worried. Jefferson's plans should "alarm all who are anxious for the safety of our government," he wrote in the *New-York Evening Post*. To a friend, privately, Hamilton confided, "Mine is an odd destiny. Perhaps no man in the United States has sacrificed and done more for the present Constitution than myself; and . . . I am still laboring to prop the frail and worthless fabric. . . . What can I do better than withdraw from the scene? Every day proves to me more and more that this American world was not meant for me."

It was not only Federalists who opposed the president. Aaron Burr, Jefferson's own vice president, was a Republican but not always an ally. Burr had, after all, wanted to be president himself, and Jefferson was wary of Burr's ambition. His vice president seemed willing to make deals with the Federalists to gain more power. "Burr will doubtless be dropped at another election, if they can do it without endangering Jefferson," a Federalist predicted.

⋙ ⋘

Jefferson wanted to extend his knowledge of the North American West. He had long worried that Britain, France, or Spain might try to settle that part of the continent, hemming in the United States and even threatening invasion. The first step toward gaining control of these lands was to explore them. He chose his own secretary, Meriwether Lewis, to lead an expedition, hoping he would find a route to the Pacific Ocean and bring back an account of all the lands he would cross along the way.

"Capt. Lewis is brave, prudent, habituated to [used to] the woods, and familiar with Indian manners and character," Jefferson said. Congress secretly agreed to pay for the mission. The president asked for twenty-five hundred dollars; the expedition ended up costing about fifteen times that amount. Lewis asked William Clark to join him in leading what became known as the Corps of Volunteers for North West Discovery.

Jefferson thought of America as an "empire of liberty." Now he would have a keener, more detailed grasp of the continent stretching far beyond the nation's existing borders—and a chance at claiming that sprawling West.

Charles Willson Peale's portraits of Meriwether Lewis and William Clark, leaders of the expedition to western North America.

CHAPTER NINETEEN

The Air of Enchantment!

Every face wears a smile, and every heart leaps with joy.
—Andrew Jackson

Jefferson had broad power to shape the country as he pleased as president, and he used that power freely, waging a war against piracy, removing judges and other political officers from power, exploring the West. Not everyone appreciated his actions. He received a letter stating the writer's hopes "that your Excellency might be beheaded within one year." Another anonymous writer told Jefferson that he had been asked "to go to Washington and then assassinate you."

James Callender chose another way to attack the president. On Wednesday, September 1, 1802, he published an article in the Richmond *Recorder*, revealing the relationship between Thomas Jefferson and Sally Hemings.

It is well known that the man, whom it delighteth the people to honor, keeps, and for many years past has kept, as his concubine, one of his own slaves. Her name is SALLY. . . . By this wench Sally, our president has had several children. There is not an individual in the neighborhood of Charlottesville who does not believe the story; and not a few who know it. . . . When Mr. Jefferson has read this article, he will find leisure to estimate how much has been lost or gained by so many unprovoked attacks upon J. T. CALLENDER.

An issue of *The Recorder* published by Henry Pace and James T. Callender in Richmond, Virginia, in 1802.

Not long afterward, Callender was found drowned in three feet of water in the James River on a day when he had been seen wandering drunkenly through Richmond. There was no evidence of murder; it was a pathetic end to a tragic life.

"Callender and Sally will be remembered as long as Jefferson as blots upon his character," wrote John Adams. "The story . . . is a natural and almost unavoidable consequence of that foul contagion [sickness] in the human character, Negro slavery."

Jefferson himself never responded directly to Callender's article. When Patsy and a secretary later showed him a poem from a different newspaper that mentioned Sally Hemings, he laughed them off but did not discuss it. So far as historians know, no one in his family or circle of friends ever raised the question with him again. It seemed that Jefferson believed in a code of silence about his relationship. He did not break that silence.

⚜ ⚜

Jefferson's family came to Washington for Christmas in 1802. Margaret Bayard Smith, a close friend of Jefferson's, spent a good deal of time with both Patsy and Polly. She found Polly to be "beautiful, simplicity and timidity personified when in company, but when alone with you of communicative and winning manners." As for Patsy, Smith found her "rather homely [plain], a delicate likeness of her father, but still more interesting. . . . She is really one of the most lovely women I have ever met with, her countenance beaming with intelligence, benevolence, and her conversation fulfills all her countenance promises. Her manners, so frank and affectionate, that you know her at once, and feel perfectly at your ease with her."

Margaret Bayard Smith, a writer based in Washington, D.C., was a friend of Thomas Jefferson's. Her letters and notebooks provide an intimate look at life in the capital.

Jefferson loved it when his whole family was with him. A caller once found the president sitting on the drawing room floor in the midst of grandchildren, "so eagerly and noisily engaged in a game of romps" that he did not notice his visitor for a moment. And he missed his children and grandchildren when they were gone. "Adieu once more," Polly wrote her father once they had left for home. "How much I think of you at the hours which we have been accustomed to be with you alone, my dear Papa."

Despite it all—the attacks from Callender, the toll of governing, the loneliness of the President's House—Jefferson liked being president. He was driven by a need to keep the United States safe from all enemies, those abroad and those at home. Most leaders can only hope to shape their nation for a brief time. In the middle of 1803, a report from Paris would give Jefferson the power to transform his for all time.

Rumors were flying that Spain had signed a treaty giving

France ownership of the Louisiana Territory in North America. This area of land was much larger than the state we know today as Louisiana; it covered more than eight hundred thousand square miles and was slightly larger than the United States itself as it existed in Jefferson's time.

"I am willing to hope, as long as anybody will hope with me," that the rumors were wrong, Jefferson said. But they were not. Napoleon, the new emperor of France, now had a vast interest in, and on, the American continent.

NAPOLEON BONAPARTE

A general in the French army, Napoleon Bonaparte seized power in 1799, when he was thirty years old. He steadily increased his influence over the government until he was crowned the emperor of France. The country that had executed its king was now led by a dictator.

Hungry for more power, Napoleon carried on wars with Italy, Austria, Spain, Russia, and Great Britain, until it seemed possible that much of Europe would fall under his rule. But after the destruction of Napoleon's navy at the Battle of Trafalgar and a disastrous invasion of Russia, the other European nations united against France. Napoleon was eventually forced to abdicate, or give up his throne, in 1814. After attempting to regain control of his country, he was finally defeated at the Battle of Waterloo in 1815. Jefferson, however, could not have known of Napoleon's future downfall. During his presidency, the emperor of France was a very real and alarming threat.

Painting of Napoleon Bonaparte by Jacques-Louis David. Napoleon's decision to sell the Louisiana Territory to Jefferson transformed the United States forever.

"There is on the globe one single spot, the possessor of which is our natural and habitual [regular] enemy. It is New Orleans," Jefferson stated. New Orleans, where the Mississippi River flows into the sea, was a vital port for American crops on their way to market. Anyone who controlled this port would have control over too much of America for Jefferson to feel at ease.

Under My Wings Everything Prospers is a painting of 1803 New Orleans by John L. Boqueta de Woiseri. It celebrates the prosperity that the Port of New Orleans brought to the United States after the Louisiana Purchase.

Jefferson had been willing to tolerate the Spanish as neighbors; the Spanish empire was not as powerful or as aggressive as France under the lead of Napoleon Bonaparte. "Spain might have retained it [New Orleans] quietly for years," Jefferson said. "Not so can it ever be in the hands of France." There could be only one outcome, as far as Jefferson was concerned: "The day that France takes possession of New Orleans . . . we must marry ourselves to the British fleet and nation," since the British were Napoleon's bitterest enemies.

Jefferson approached the moment with confidence. He knew he needed to control the way decisions would be made,

Portrait of James Monroe, Jefferson's ally and protégé. Jefferson trusted Monroe to go to France to negotiate the Louisiana Purchase.

a lesson learned in Williamsburg during the debates over the Stamp Act. So he sent his own messenger, James Monroe, to Paris. He knew he needed to rally the public with words, a lesson learned while writing the Declaration of Independence. And, most important, he knew he could not hesitate but must seize the right moment to act, a lesson learned in his days as governor of Virginia during the Revolution.

Before James Monroe had even reached Paris, events were unfolding there. Napoleon was on the verge of declaring war against England. With such battles close to home, holding and defending lands in North America would become too expensive and troublesome. Napoleon made the decision Jefferson had hoped he would make: to sell Louisiana.

While the emperor was in his bath, soaking in water sweet with cologne, his brothers came in to protest the decision. "You will have no need to lead the opposition," Napoleon told them, "for I repeat there will be no debate, for the reason that the project . . . conceived by me, negotiated by me, shall be ratified and executed by me, alone. Do you comprehend me?"

"I renounce Louisiana," Napoleon announced on April 11, 1803. "It is not only New Orleans that I will cede [give up], it is the whole colony without any reservation. I know the price of what I abandon. . . . I renounce it with the greatest regret. But to attempt obstinately to retain it would be folly." Within hours, his foreign minister was inquiring whether the United States would be interested in buying the territory.

James Monroe and Robert R. Livingston (the American minister already in Paris) knew that they could not miss this chance. They negotiated a treaty giving the Louisiana Territory to the United States. The territory more than doubled the size of the country; it was so large that neither the buyers nor the sellers were quite clear about the borders. (The question of whether the United States had bought Florida wouldn't be settled for many years.) The price was fifteen million dollars, or three cents an acre.

Word reached Jefferson on a Sunday evening. He was stunned—happily. "It is something larger than the whole U.S., containing 500 millions of acres, the U.S. containing 434 millions," he wrote. "This removes from us the greatest source of danger to our peace." The territory purchased in this deal today makes up all or part of the states of Louisiana, Arkansas, Oklahoma, Texas, Missouri, Kansas, Colorado, Iowa, Nebraska, Wyoming, Minnesota, South Dakota, North Dakota, and Montana.

Map outlining the boundaries of the Louisiana Purchase.

"It must . . . strike the mind of every true friend to freedom in the United States, as the greatest and most beneficial event that has taken place since the Declaration of Independence," wrote an army general. "It has the air of enchantment!" The future president Andrew Jackson wrote to Jefferson from the West, saying, "Every face wears a smile, and every heart leaps with joy."

To be legal, the treaty that Monroe and Livingston had negotiated needed to be ratified, or approved, by Congress. Jefferson asked the lawmakers to meet on what he called "great and weighty matters." Word had reached Jefferson from Paris: Monroe and Livingston warned that France was growing uncomfortable with the deal. Fearing trouble, Jefferson pressed for a quick vote. As was so often the case, he got what he wanted. The treaty was ratified. Louisiana was now part of the United States.

Jefferson's decision to acquire Louisiana expanded the powers of the presidency in ways that would likely have driven him to distraction had another man been

The treaty that granted the transfer of Louisiana from France to the United States.

president. Nothing in the Constitution gave the president power to sign treaties such as this one. Jefferson himself thought at first that what he had done would require an amendment to the Constitution, but he quickly changed his mind. There was no time for that, with France possibly regretting the treaty and looking for any excuse to take its territory back. Jefferson did what had to be done, and quickly, to preserve the security of the United States, to preserve the ideals of democracy and progress.

The story of the Louisiana Purchase is one of strength. By buying the territory, Jefferson doubled the size of the country and made the United States into a power to be reckoned with by anyone who might hope to stake a claim on the North American continent. A slower or less courageous politician might have bungled the purchase; one who was too idealistic might have lost it by insisting on a constitutional amendment. Jefferson, however, was neither slow nor weak nor too idealistic.

As Jefferson crafted the deal, he took some time to write to Meriwether Lewis, who left Washington on Tuesday, July 5, beginning the expedition that would take him and his party up the Mississippi River, through present-day North Dakota, and along the Columbia River to the Pacific. Thanks to the Louisiana Purchase, much of the territory they would be exploring would soon be part of the United States.

Jefferson had written instructions, offered advice, and worried over details. Now the journey was in the hands of the explorers, and the president waited eagerly for news.

Lewis and Clark holding council with the Native Americans they met during their exploration of the Louisiana Territory.

CHAPTER TWENTY

The People Were Never More Happy

If we can keep the vessel of state as steadily in her course for another four years, my earthly purposes will be accomplished.
—THOMAS JEFFERSON

On most afternoons when he was in Washington, Jefferson received his dinner guests at the President's House around three or four o'clock. He entertained constantly, handsomely, and with a purpose. His instinct to open his house and table was natural, something he had learned growing up in the world of Virginia hospitality.

Spending time with his fellows was not only pleasant for Jefferson; he believed it was essential for life in the United States. Men who liked and respected each other would be good citizens of a republic. They would be more likely to make sacrifices for each other, to listen to each other, and to compromise when needed.

Jefferson gathered lawmakers, diplomats, and government officials around his table for a more practical reason as well. It was more difficult to oppose—or at least to attack—someone with whom you had broken bread or drunk wine. Jefferson knew that when you eat dessert with a fellow politician, even one whose opinions you dislike, you see him as a person— not as an evil force to destroy.

To Jefferson, each guest who came into his house was important, and he had little patience—no patience, in fact—for the trappings of rank. He did away with the formal seating that Washington and Adams had practiced, allowing guests to choose their own places at his table. When the wife of a British diplomat objected angrily, feeling that she and her husband had not received the respect they were due, Jefferson said simply, "The principle of society with us . . . is the equal rights of all." He also put an end to the formal and tedious drinking of toasts to the president's health, preferring free-flowing conversation.

One guest described his first dinner at the President's House to his wife. The food "was excellent, cooked rather in the French style (larded venison), the dessert was profuse and extremely elegant. . . . Wine in great variety, from sherry to champagne, and a few decanters of rare Spanish wine." At first, Jefferson hung back, playing the host; then he joined the stream of talk brilliantly.

"It is a long time since I have been present at so elegant a mental treat," his guest wrote. "Literature, wit, and a little business, with a great deal of miscellaneous remarks on agriculture and building, filled every minute. There is a degree of ease in Mr. Jefferson's company that everyone seems to feel and enjoy."

There were some, however, who were not charmed by Jefferson. The Federalists began to grow desperate as the president's popularity grew. In February 1804, Timothy Pickering, a Federalist senator, wrote to a friend of his unhappiness under Jefferson's leadership. "And must we submit to these evils?" he wondered. "Is there no remedy?"

The most obvious remedy, to Pickering, was secession, splitting the country in two. If Massachusetts could be convinced to leave the Union, he thought, Connecticut would follow, and so would New Hampshire, Rhode Island, and Vermont. If New York believed that it would be the center of a new country, that state would follow, he said, which would bring along New Jersey and perhaps part of Pennsylvania. "It is not unusual for two friends when disagreeing . . . to separate, and manage each in his own way his separate interest,"

Pickering wrote. It all seemed so reasonable, but it would have meant civil war.

Nothing came of Pickering's scheme, but rumors of secession persisted for several years. Meanwhile, Jefferson had to deal with his vice president. Jefferson and Aaron Burr had had little contact for the first four years of the presidency. In 1804, Jefferson was facing a new election, and he was determined to keep Burr off the ballot this time. Burr met with the president and offered to stay out of the election, but he asked for Jefferson to give him something else—an appointment to a government job. Jefferson refused. He did not want to be seen as bribing or bargaining with anyone to enter the election or stay out of it. He could do nothing, he said, for his vice president.

Meanwhile, the states were in the process of approving the Twelfth Amendment to the Constitution, which would require electors to cast separate votes for the offices of vice president and president. This would prevent any ties for the office of the president, as Jefferson and Burr had experienced in their first election.

❧ ❧

Polly gave birth to a daughter on February 15, 1804. All was not well. "I feel dreadfully apprehensive," her husband confided in Jefferson. Jefferson left Washington for Monticello in April, and when he arrived, he found Polly much worse than he expected. He immediately took charge of her care.

Thirteen days after her father reached home, Polly died. "How the President will get over this blow I cannot pronounce," Patsy's husband wrote. "He passed all last evening with his handkerchief in his hand."

Exhausted and grieving, Jefferson returned to Washington. On June 2, an unexpected letter arrived for him. It was from Abigail Adams.

For a long time, she wrote, she had not believed there was any event that could make her sympathize with the man who had once been her close friend and was now a bitter political enemy. "But I know how closely entwined around a parent's heart, are those cords which bind" a parent to a child, she told him. And she knew "how agonizing the pangs of separation."

Jefferson answered the letter politely. He and Abigail wrote six more letters, but it became clear that their views of current and past events were so different that further conversation was pointless. John Adams knew nothing of his wife's letters to Jefferson until after the last had been exchanged.

On Wednesday, July 11, 1804, the vice president of the United States shot and killed a man. The dead man was Alexander Hamilton, the first secretary of the Treasury and Thomas Jefferson's most hated political enemy.

A depiction of the duel between Aaron Burr and Alexander Hamilton, which resulted in Hamilton's death.

Aaron Burr held Hamilton at least partly responsible for the fact that he had lost a race for governor of New York and had not been selected to run for a second term as vice president. Enraged, he challenged Hamilton to a duel, and Hamilton accepted. After they exchanged bullets, Burr was still alive, but Hamilton was dead. Jefferson's vice president had killed his bitterest political rival.

The president kept silent about the entire situation. He offered no tribute to Hamilton's long service in the government. Perhaps he worried that, with an election coming up, any praise of Hamilton would be taken as support for his politics. And that Jefferson could not risk. He still disagreed with nearly everything Hamilton had stood for. "Each of us, perhaps, thought well of the other as a man," Jefferson admitted later, "but as politicians it was impossible for two men to be of more opposite principles."

The more pressing issue for Jefferson was his vice president. Aaron Burr had been charged with murder in both New York and New Jersey. By the end of July, he had escaped both states. In fact, he left the eastern United States entirely and made his way to the West.

With Burr gone, the Republicans chose George Clinton of New York as the Republican candidate for vice president in the upcoming election. Clinton was the child of Irish immigrants. John Jay, a Federalist, grumbled that "Clinton's family and connections do not entitle him" to such a distinguished job, but Jefferson's view was different. His philosophy allowed and encouraged white men to rise up through the social ranks by their own abilities.

The Federalist candidate was Charles Cotesworth Pinckney, but he had little chance. Jefferson's popularity, based on lower taxes, a time of prosperity, and the Louisiana Purchase, was secure. He was elected with 162 electoral votes; Pinckney got 14.

George Clinton of New York succeeded Burr as vice president for Jefferson's second presidential term.

"All is now business, hurry, interruption," Jefferson wrote on the eve of his second inauguration. The day itself fell on a Monday. Jefferson rose, dressed in black, and left the grounds of the President's House on horseback. In the Senate, again speaking too softly to be widely heard, Jefferson gave his second inaugural address. Then he returned to the President's House, which was open to everyone who chose to come and celebrate the beginning of his second term.

He did not intend to try for another. "Genl. Washington set the example of voluntary retirement after 8 years. I shall follow it," he wrote. But he could imagine one circumstance under which he would try to stay in power: if he thought there was a chance of "a monarchist" winning the next election. "But this circumstance is impossible," he added.

In the spring of 1805, the first news from the Lewis and Clark expedition arrived. William Clark sent Jefferson the notes he had kept on their journey so far, in the form of a journal. Captain Lewis wrote that he had "hopes of complete success."

Camped for the winter on the Missouri River in North Dakota, Lewis and Clark sent Jefferson a box with the skins and skeletons of antelope and weasels and wolves, elk horns, plants, and four living magpies. Jefferson was delighted.

News of the expedition fascinated the public. "The voyage of discovery of Capt. Lewis has engaged the attention of the curious and attracted the notice of many," one commentator

THE CORPS OF DISCOVERY

Captain Meriwether Lewis, Lieutenant William Clark, and the men of the Corps of Discovery traveled nearly eight thousand miles. Leaving from Illinois on May 14, 1804, they followed the Missouri River upstream, crossed the Bitterroot Mountains (helped greatly by their Shoshone guide and interpreter, Sacagawea), and arrived at the Pacific Ocean on December 3, 1805.

Lewis and Clark followed their instructions from Jefferson to take detailed notes of everything they found—plants, animals, soil, climate, Native American tribes. Lewis described 178 plants and 122 animals that had not been known to science before, including the grizzly bear and the prairie dog. They did not, however, discover the Northwest Passage, an all-water route connecting the Atlantic to the Pacific, which had been one of Jefferson's fondest hopes.

A mural by Edgar Samuel Paxson depicting Lewis and Clark with Sacagawea.

wrote. "This nation was never more respected abroad. The people were never more happy at home."

In late 1805, Lewis and his company achieved the success he had hoped for. On a tree overlooking the Pacific, Clark staked the claim Jefferson had long dreamed of:

> *Capt William Clark*
> *December 3, 1805.*
> *By Land.*
> *U States in 1804 & 1805*

A mission begun on the Potomac had ended by the Pacific. It was a staggering achievement.

Under Jefferson, the President's House slowly filled with artifacts and curiosities, such as those sent to him by Lewis

Reconstructed site of Fort Clatsop, the last encampment of the Corps of Discovery.

and Clark. The building was becoming something it had not been before: a center of inquiry, a place for science, literature, and discovery.

Jefferson set aside a room for fossils. There were pieces of skulls, jawbones, teeth, tusks, a foreleg, "one horn of a colossal animal," and two hundred small bones collected by William Clark. An explorer in the Southwest bought two bear cubs for Jefferson, and they arrived safely at the President's House in 1808. "I would recommend . . . that they should be confined together in a cell (without chains) and regularly supplied with food and water," he suggested.

Jefferson took the advice. "I put them together while here in a place 10 f. square," he wrote. "For the first day they worried one another very much with play, but after that they played at times, but were extremely happy together." In the end, the cubs were sent to a zoo in Philadelphia.

A British diplomat wrote of Jefferson that he "is well-placed to be considered as an able statesman; but he is still more proud of being thought to combine a capacity for public affairs with . . . scientific pursuit."

But he could not spend much time on science. In 1805, Jefferson was dealing with Spain over the exact borders of the Louisiana Purchase. Was Florida part of the Louisiana Purchase? Or was it still Spain's territory? This had never

Charles Marion Russell's painting re-creates Lewis and Clark's voyage on the lower Columbia River. The Corps of Discovery's journey to the Pacific was a crowning achievement of the Jefferson presidency.

been entirely clear, and it would not be settled until 1819, well after Jefferson's presidency. Jefferson considered using force against Spain's territory in North America but decided that the United States was safer staying out of battles. "Our constitution is a peace establishment—it is not calculated for war," he said. "War would endanger its existence."

As 1805 drew to a close, Jefferson saw enemies wherever he looked. The British and the French were harassing American ships on the seas. England and France were bitterly at war. Jefferson's old vice president, Aaron Burr, was rumored to be plotting against the United States.

"What an awful spectacle does the world exhibit at this instant," Jefferson wrote in 1806. He hoped that the United States could stay out of the devastating European wars and be "quiet, at home at least." But he had to face the question: How long would the quiet last? How long *could* it last?

CHAPTER TWENTY-ONE

A Deep, Dark, and Widespread Conspiracy

Never since the battle of Lexington have I seen this country in such a state of exasperation as present.
—THOMAS JEFFERSON

Jefferson's winter was brightened by a long visit from Patsy, his only surviving daughter from his marriage to Patty. While staying in the President's House, Patsy gave birth to a son, James Madison Randolph, named in honor of his grandfather's friend. Dolley Madison, James's wife, helped Patsy prepare for life in Washington, buying "a fashionable wig . . . a set of combs for dressing the hair, a bonnet, shawl, and white lace veil from Baltimore, as well as two lace handkerchiefs."

In the summer, there was something new—a serious drought in Virginia. In the autumn, something by now familiar—reports that Aaron Burr was making trouble.

Since the duel with Hamilton, Burr had been wandering over the country. Rumors drifted east that Burr was trying to persuade various states to break away from the country or was planning to attack Mexico. The worst reports suggested that Burr was gathering soldiers, collecting weapons, and building boats in preparation for a march on Washington, D.C.

"This is indeed a deep, dark and widespread conspiracy," a general wrote to Jefferson in November. "I fear it will receive strong support in New Orleans."

What exactly was Burr doing? It is not certain even now. He did seem to be preparing for an expedition of some kind, although it is not clear what his goal was. Possibly he meant to attack Texas, then a part of Spanish-controlled Mexico. Jefferson certainly believed that Burr meant to seize control over land somewhere in the West, perhaps hoping to form an empire of his own.

Jefferson drafted a bill for Congress, asking it to grant him power to use the army or the navy "in cases of insurrection," or rebellion. (He did not want to appear power hungry, however, and asked an ally in Congress to copy the bill in the lawmaker's own handwriting and submit it as his own idea. It was pure political Jefferson—to achieve power but to keep his own role in doing so disguised.)

By late March 1807, Burr was under arrest. He was brought to Richmond for trial. The charge was not the murder of Alexander Hamilton but treason against the United States of America. John Marshall was the judge who presided over the case. Jefferson followed the trial in detail, advising the lawyer who presented the case against Burr. But when this lawyer sent a messenger to Jefferson, requiring him to appear as a witness against the former vice president, Jefferson refused to leave the President's House.

Portrait of Aaron Burr.

"I do not believe that the district courts have a power of *commanding* the Executive government to abandon superior duties and attend on them," Jefferson wrote back. He called the idea "preposterous." The president, Jefferson was saying, had a job so important that he could not leave it even when summoned to bear witness in court. But he did agree to send the documents that the lawyer needed. This compromise meant that Jefferson could avoid claiming that the president was above the law.

AARON BURR AND ALEXANDER HAMILTON

Aaron Burr never went to prison for the murder of Alexander Hamilton. After being found innocent of treason (to Thomas Jefferson's disgust), Burr left the United States for Europe, where he lived for four years. He contacted Napoleon and tried to interest the emperor of France in invading Florida, with no success. Burr finally returned to New York, where he worked as a lawyer until his death in 1836.

Eventually, Burr was found not guilty of treason. The evidence against him was weak. He had clearly killed Hamilton, but it was not as obvious that he was planning to wage war on the United States. Jefferson was enraged and blamed his cousin John Marshall for the verdict. "The nation will judge both the offender and the judges for themselves," he wrote.

He had been miserable for a week. He had another headache, which made it difficult for him to work. "I am now in the 7th day of a periodical head-ache," he wrote to Patsy. "The fits are by no means as severe as I have felt in former times, but they hold me back very long, from 9 or 10 in the morning till dark." There were also the usual complaints and stresses. "I am tired of an office where I can do no more good than many others who would be glad to be employed in it," he wrote to an old friend.

Tensions with England were growing. The British insisted that they had the right to search American ships they encountered on the seas, in case deserters from the British navy were among their crews. Americans resented the searches. In July 1807, a crisis erupted. A British ship, the HMS *Leopard,* demanded to search an American ship, the

USS *Chesapeake*. When the American captain of the *Chesapeake* refused to allow the search, the British captain opened fire. Three men were killed; the *Chesapeake*'s commanding officer and seventeen others were wounded.

Painting of the USS *Chesapeake*, 1814.

It was an act of war—an insult to, and an attack on, the United States of America. The public was outraged. Jefferson issued a proclamation banning armed British ships from American waters. He told the states to make their militias ready and ordered weapons, ammunition, and supplies. He did this without the approval of Congress, since the lawmakers were not together to vote. It was an act that strengthened the defense of the country *and* the power of the president.

A ship was sent to England to receive an answer from the British government about the *Leopard*'s attack. While he waited, Jefferson calmly prepared for the possibility of war. But he was in no hurry. He knew that America could not quickly build a navy to compete with England's. The country's best hope, he believed, was to allow time to pass. If England would apologize for the attack on the *Chesapeake,* all might yet be well.

England did not. Far from making any apology, King George III ordered all British ships to seize British sailors from ships belonging to any other country. French emperor Napoleon, meanwhile, announced that he expected all countries, including the United States, to ban imports from his archenemy, England.

America seemed caught between two great powers of Europe. Jefferson proposed that the United States order its own ships to remain in port and was "making every preparation for whatever events may grow out of the present crisis."

What came next? Politically, war seemed impossible. The answer was an embargo, or a ban on all goods, against England. It was far from ideal. "Governmental prohibitions do always more mischief than had been calculated," Jefferson's secretary of the Treasury told him. A politician should not be quick to "regulate the concerns of individuals as if he could do it better than themselves."

Jefferson agreed in theory, but he was practical. The embargo was, for the moment, the best of several bad choices. It would buy time, and he still felt that time was America's best ally. "This gives time. Time may produce peace in Europe," he wrote. "Peace in Europe removes all causes of differences till another European war."

On December 22, 1807, Jefferson signed the Embargo Act. It was a breathtaking expansion of governmental power. Trade with foreign nations was forbidden. Nothing could come into the country; nothing could go out.

The embargo turned American politics upside down. Republicans, including Jefferson, had once fought to limit the power of the national government, to keep the president from making himself into a king. By signing this bill, Jefferson was announcing that the national government (with him as the president) had the power to control the economic life of every American.

Was the embargo a success? In some ways, no. It caused hardship for many people who needed goods they could not buy. It delayed, but it did not prevent, war with Great Britain. The tensions that sparked the embargo would eventually lead to the War of 1812. But the embargo did allow Jefferson to avoid, for the moment, a war for which he felt the United States was not prepared.

Jefferson tried to convince himself that the embargo was working. "I have been happy in my journey through the country to this place to find the people unanimous in their preference of the embargo to war," he wrote from Monticello in May 1808.

His own mail, however, suggested how painful and frustrating the embargo was for many. "You infernal villain," one man wrote from Boston. "How much longer are you going to keep this damned Embargo on to starve us poor people. One of my children has already starved to death. . . . I have three more children which I expect will starve soon if I don't get something for them to eat which cannot be had."

There was more talk of some of the states breaking away from the Union. The governor of Massachusetts warned Jefferson that "the attempt is . . . to divide the nation" and set up "a different form of government, under the protection of Great Britain." He added, "You will laugh at this, and so would Southern members of Congress, but their destruction will come upon them."

Jefferson's opponents did not need to split the country to express their displeasure with him and with the embargo. A simpler method was at hand—the presidential election of 1808. Jefferson had no intention of running for a third term. He hoped that his good friend and ally James Madison might follow him into the office. The Federalists once again proposed Charles Cotesworth Pinckney.

Madison was seen as Jefferson's follower, and the election was a judgment on Jefferson's time in office. Familiar themes were repeated in the campaign—that Madison favored the French and disliked the British, that Virginia had held power for too long, that leaving the Republicans in power would lead to mob rule.

Nothing worked. Madison won 122 electoral votes to Pinckney's 47.

Portrait of Charles Cotesworth Pinckney, who ran against James Madison in the presidential election of 1808.

CHAPTER TWENTY-TWO

A Farewell to Ultimate Power

Amidst the din of war and the wreck of nations his wisdom has hitherto secured our peace.
—TOAST TO THOMAS JEFFERSON AT THE TAMMANY SOCIETY OF WASHINGTON, MAY 12, 1809

"I am already sensible [aware] of decay in the power of walking, and find my memory not so faithful as it used to be," Thomas Jefferson wrote an old friend on Christmas Day 1808. He had been at this for so long. It was time to go home.

As he made lists of his furniture in the President's House and thought about how to pay his bills (he was in debt for roughly eight to ten thousand dollars after his years as president), he knew an age was coming to an end. This age had lasted more than forty years, through war and peace, at home and abroad, from Williamsburg and Richmond to Philadelphia and New York and Annapolis and Paris and London and finally to Washington, D.C.

He had, he believed, done his duty. "Nature intended me for the tranquil pursuit of science," he wrote. "But the enormities of the times in which I have lived" had forced him into politics.

Jefferson's victory in the election of 1800 had, as he saw it, saved the United States from the designs of the Federalists and those determined to change the new democracy back into a monarchy. It had been his great work to put a stop to this plan, and this had laid him open to criticism and complaint from his enemies. In his view, Jefferson had become "of course the butt of everything which reason, ridicule, malice, and falsehood could supply."

But there was praise as well. On the day before James Madison became president, the *National Intelligencer* published a tribute to the departing president. "Never will it be forgotten as long as liberty is dear to man," it said, "that it was on this day that Thomas Jefferson retired" from the office of president of the United States.

James Madison taking the presidential oath of office in 1809.

On the morning of James Madison's inauguration, Jefferson left the President's House and rode up to the Capitol to watch his friend and secretary of state take the oath as the fourth president of the United States. No one on earth was closer to Jefferson politically. Madison's election was a sign that the country overall approved of Jefferson's vision and his work as president.

After the ceremony, Jefferson called on the new president at his home. Mrs. Madison looked "extremely beautiful," a friend remarked, "dressed in a plain cambric dress with a very long train . . . all dignity, grace, and affability [kindness]."

Jefferson saw his old friend Margaret Bayard Smith and reached for her hand.

"Remember the promise you have made me, to come to see us next summer, do not forget it," he said to Mrs. Smith, "for we shall certainly expect you."

Mrs. Smith promised him that she and her husband would come to Monticello. "You have now resigned a heavy burden," she said to Jefferson.

"Yes indeed," he answered, "and am much happier at this moment than my friend."

At Monticello, he planned to return to farming and gardening. "I am full of plans of employment when I get there," he wrote. "An only daughter and numerous family of grandchildren will furnish me great resources of happiness."

He had suggested that perhaps his sister Anne Scott Marks could act as mistress of Monticello. Patsy hated the thought. She—and no one else—would manage her father's house. "As to Aunt Marks it would not be desirable to have her," Patsy wrote firmly.

> *I had full proof of her being totally incom[petent] to the business the last summer. The servants have no sort of respect for her and take just what they please before her face. She is an excellent creature and a neat manager in a little way, but she has neither head nor a sufficient weight of character to manage so large an establishment as yours will be. I shall devote myself to it and with feeling, which I never could have in my own affairs, and with what tenderness of affection we will wait upon and cherish you My Dearest Father.*

On Wednesday, March 15, 1809, Thomas Jefferson reached Monticello. He brought the great world with him. His chef came to set up the Monticello kitchen and to prepare the French dishes Jefferson loved. The books he read and the letters he wrote and received were many and varied. Home to stay, he was never again to stray very far from his mountaintop. His mind was another matter. It never came to rest.

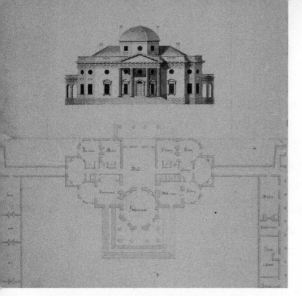

A plan for Monticello by architect Robert Mills. Jefferson worked on renovating Monticello from the time of his retirement from George Washington's administration through his own presidency. Completed in 1809, it bore little resemblance to Mills's sketch.

In his rooms at Monticello, Jefferson slept on a bed built into an alcove between his study (which was often called his "cabinet") and a chamber with a fireplace. Red bed curtains hung on each side of the bed. A 1790 clock rested on a wooden shelf inside his sleeping alcove; it chimed with a delicate ting on the hour and the half hour. Below the clock hung a sword—the gift, it was said, of "a long forgotten Arabian prince." And there were always the sounds of Jefferson's pet mockingbirds.

Jefferson had his own privy, or bathroom, just steps away from his bed alcove; it was one of three in the house. He used pieces of paper for cleanliness. (Some of the unused pieces were collected by a member of his family on the day of his death and are now kept in the Library of Congress.)

He generally got five to eight hours of sleep a night, always reading for half an hour or an hour before bed. The windows of his chambers faced east and received the first light of the morning. He would sit up in his alcove and turn to his left to plunge his feet into a basin of cold water. There he would sit for a time, looking at the fireplace and tracking the rise of the sun.

The house where he woke every morning was his joy. And it was only in the years after he retired from the presidency that the house was exactly as he wished it to be.

Walking into the entrance hall, Jefferson, his family, and his guests were immediately surrounded by the work of his life. There were the antlers of moose and elk, the upper jawbone of a mastodon, and forty objects from Native American tribes, including carved stone sculptures, tools, and a buffalo robe. There was a map of Virginia drawn by his father, and more of North America, Europe, Africa, and Asia. There was a scale model of the Pyramid of Cheops.

There were also paintings, including one of Jesus and one of Saint Jerome, portraits of John Adams and Jefferson, an engraving of the Declaration of Independence, and busts of Alexander Hamilton and Jefferson.

Nothing was random. The portraits, statues, and artifacts in the house were "memorials of those worthies," Jefferson said, who brought him "pride and comfort." Anything or anyone represented in Monticello was meaningful to Jefferson.

Jefferson's bedchamber at Monticello.

While in Paris, Jefferson ordered copies made of several portraits of critical figures in American history, including this one of Christopher Columbus.

Jefferson admired Sir Walter Raleigh's exploration of the New World.

Guests moved through the hall, beneath the tall ceiling and across a beautiful floor of cherry and beech, with a pattern designed by Jefferson himself, to reach the parlor, with its card tables, chairs, sofas, chess set, harpsichord, and piano. Here hung paintings and sculptures of the makers of the age, and of all ages—George Washington, Benjamin Franklin, Napoleon, Lafayette, Christopher Columbus, Sir Walter Raleigh, James Madison, Thomas Paine, James Monroe, Louis XVI, Sir Isaac Newton, John Adams, and Jefferson himself.

The brilliant yellow dining room was to the right. Patsy had a blue sitting room near her father's private rooms. The upstairs was a series of small bedrooms. The center of the house, and the center of life, was downstairs, where Jefferson was always at the center of everything.

Jefferson's "cheerfulness and affection," a granddaughter recalled, "were the warm sun in which his family all basked." His grandchildren loved and were a little in awe of him. They followed him on garden walks (never daring to put a foot off the path and onto a garden bed, for that would break one of his rules). He never needed "to utter a harsh word to one of us, or speak in a raised tone of voice, or use a threat," one granddaughter recalled. "He simply said, 'do,' or 'do not.'" And that was that.

Jefferson also admired Sir Isaac Newton's scientific mind.

He picked fruit for the grandchildren—usually figs or cherries—with a long stick topped with a hook and a net bag. He organized races across the terrace or over the lawns, giving the younger children head starts. Awards were three figs, prunes, or dates for first place, two for second, and one for third. On some summer nights, he set up a chess table outside—he had designed it himself, and John Hemings had made it—for matches with a granddaughter.

In the wintertime, Jefferson would sit with his family before a fire in the afternoon. "When it grew too dark to read," a granddaughter remembered, and before candles were brought in, "as we all sat round the fire, he taught us several childish games, and would play them with us."

The arrival of candles signaled an end to games. Everything fell quiet as Jefferson picked up his book once more. "We would not speak out of a whisper lest we should disturb him," remembered one of his grandchildren. "Generally we followed his example and took a book—and I have seen him raise his eyes from his own book and look round on the little circle of readers, and smile and make some remark to mamma about it."

He once overheard a young granddaughter lament that she had never had a silk dress. One arrived for her from Charlottesville the next day. Another time, he saw a granddaughter tear her beloved muslin dress on a door. Several days later,

Jefferson came into Patsy's sitting room, "a bundle in his hand." To his granddaughter, he said, "I have been mending your dress for you." It was a new frock.

Hearing a child express a wish for a watch, a saddle and bridle, or a guitar, he would quietly provide them. He made sure his grandchildren were given Bibles and Shakespeare and writing tables. "Our grandfather seemed to read our hearts, to see our invisible wishes . . . to wave the fairy wand, to brighten our young lives by his goodness and his gifts," one grandchild remembered.

His sense of the needs of others was part of his nature. As a politician and as the head of a family, he had always figured out what others wanted and needed, and he tried, within reason, to provide it. That had been the work of Jefferson's public life, and now it was that of his personal life, too.

The entrance at Monticello.

On her promised visit to Monticello, in the middle of 1809, Margaret Bayard Smith thought Jefferson in a perfect place and frame of mind. "The sun never sees him in bed, and his mind designs more than the day can fulfill, even his long day," she wrote. "There is a tranquility about him, which an inward peace could alone bestow."

He enjoyed reading of the public's confidence in him. "Though I am convinced that Mr. Madison, your friend and your student, will govern according to the same principles as you have, I cannot help regretting that you did not want to retain the presidency for four more years," one friend wrote. The world still looked to Jefferson, and to America, as symbols of hope. "What would become of mankind if republican government did not survive in your country?" asked a French letter writer. "I shudder to think of the consequences!"

Jefferson read the newspapers and kept up with events, but he spent most of his time outdoors. "I am now on horseback among my farms from an early breakfast to a last dinner, with little regard to weather," he told Lafayette. "I find it gives health to body, mind and affairs." One thing was clear as he settled into life on the mountain: he loved, he said, the "luxury of being owner of my own time."

He kept up with science and with philosophy. Madison sent the skin of a bighorn sheep from the Rocky Mountains, and Jefferson debated the origins of the potato by letter, wrote for vine cuttings to grow grapes for wine, and mused on the value of libraries. "I have often thought that nothing would do more extensive good at small expense than the establishment of a small circulating library in every county to consist of a few well-chosen books, to be lent to the people of the county under such regulations as would secure their safe return in due time," he said.

In his farm book, Jefferson recorded the fate of his crops and the details of the lives of his slaves. He coolly noted down the births of his own children with Sally Hemings. These

At Monticello, the parlor was the center of social activity and where Jefferson displayed his art collection.

children did not receive the tender care that Patsy's and Polly's boys and girls knew from their grandfather. Jefferson was apparently able to think of them as something entirely separate from his cherished life with his white family. "He was not in the habit of showing . . . fatherly affection to us as children," said Jefferson's son Madison Hemings.

It was, to say the least, an odd way to live. But Jefferson was a creature of his time and age and was not the only wealthy man to watch his own children grow up in slavery. "It is far from uncommon to see a gentleman at dinner, and his . . . offspring a slave of the master of the table," a visitor to the Carolinas from Massachusetts noted.

A page from Jefferson's farm book, written in 1783.

This was the daily reality at Monticello. Jefferson dealt with it by never acknowledging it. He lived by the code of denial that defined life in the slave-owning states. It was his plantation, his world, and he would live as he wished. Any secrets that he wanted kept would never be spoken of.

CHAPTER TWENTY-THREE

We Are to Have War Then?

Every hope from time, patience and the love of peace is exhausted.
—THOMAS JEFFERSON

On the second day of 1811, Thomas Jefferson's friend Benjamin Rush began a quiet but determined effort to bring Jefferson and John Adams to exchange letters once more. If Jefferson would make the first move, Rush promised, Adams was ready for it. "Tottering over the grave," Rush said, Adams "now leans wholly on the shoulders of his old revolutionary friends."

"The friendship of two ex-presidents that were once opposed to each other," Rush told Jefferson, would be worthwhile for everyone. "Human nature will be a gainer by it."

The closeness between Jefferson and Adams had been a victim of the fury of the 1790s. Jefferson had not forgotten the conflicts of that time, particularly the Alien and Sedition Acts. In Jefferson's mind, these had been meant "to beat down the friends to the real principles of our Constitution, to silence by terror every expression in their favor, to

Benjamin Rush was a longtime friend and colleague of Jefferson's. In 1811, he encouraged Jefferson to begin writing letters again to John Adams.

bring us into war with France and alliance with England," and finally to change the United States government into the monarchy he dreaded.

Adams, too, had his own complaints about Jefferson. When two of Jefferson's friends visited Adams, they tried to ease his resentment by repeating some of Jefferson's praise for him. "Upon repeating the complimentary remarks thus made by Mr. Jefferson, Mr. Adams not only seemed but expressed himself highly pleased," one friend remembered. Adams changed his tone, putting into words his own admiration of his old friend and enemy. "I always loved Jefferson, and still love him," he said.

These eight words were all it took for Jefferson. "This is enough for me," he wrote to Benjamin Rush. His feelings of friendship were revived. Rush sent word of this to Adams, who wrote to Jefferson on New Year's Day 1812.

In reply, Jefferson struck the right notes. "A letter from you calls up recollections very dear to my mind," he wrote. "It carries me back to the times when, beset with difficulties and dangers, we were fellow laborers in the same cause, struggling for what is most valuable to man, his right of self-government."

A friendship shattered by politics was restored. The two former presidents and aging revolutionaries exchanged thoughts and memories, ideas and questions. "So many subjects crowd upon me that I know not with which to begin," Adams wrote. And he told Jefferson, "You and I ought not to die before we have explained ourselves to each other."

Jefferson loved the letters and was content to let old conflicts rest. "With the commonplace topic of politics, we do not meddle," he told another friend. "When there are so many others on which we agree why should we introduce the only one on which we differ?"

Adams did not want to dig up old arguments, either. He was unyielding, but gracious, about their differences of opinion. "In the measures of administration I have

John Adams and Jefferson met as fellow delegates to the Second Continental Congress in Philadelphia in 1775. For the next fifty years, they alternated between being friends and foes.

neither agreed with you or Mr. Madison. Whether you or I were right" the future would judge, he told his old friend.

They debated the nature of democracy and the future of the country without bitterness or anger. Jefferson, remembering what the United States had already been through, believed that more good than bad lay ahead. "We acted in perfect harmony through a long and perilous contest for our liberty and our independence," Jefferson reminded Adams. "On the subject of the history of the American revolution, you ask who shall write it?" he wrote to his old friend in another letter. "Who can write it? And who ever will be able to write it? Nobody; except merely its external facts. All its councils, designs, and discussion . . . these, which are the life and soul of history, must forever be unknown."

By the time they died, Jefferson and Adams had exchanged a total of 329 letters. One hundred and fifty-eight of them were written after 1812.

Friendship between old enemies did not exist everywhere, however. As 1811 drew to a close, war with England seemed more and more likely. Jefferson had left the presidency hoping that peace was still possible, but that hope had faded. "We are to have war then? I believe so and that it is necessary," Jefferson wrote.

Toward the end of 1811, President James Madison sent a war-preparation message to Congress. He argued that English attacks along U.S. borders and on the oceans were too much to bear. The time had come to put the question of America's continued independence to the test.

Jefferson offered warm words to Madison. "Your message had all the qualities it should possess, firm, rational, and dignified," he wrote. "Heaven help you through all your difficulties."

Jefferson had been here before. The king's army was on the move, and the American cause was in jeopardy. The conflict that began with the Declaration of Independence was rising once again. The British had never entirely accepted the idea that America was its own nation. And America knew it.

War came between Britain and America for the second time in Jefferson's life.

The War of 1812 was disastrous for the Americans. In August 1814, the British burned Washington. The President's House itself was in flames, and the First Lady, Dolley

General Andrew Jackson leads his troops in the Battle of New Orleans during the War of 1812.

Madison, saved precious documents and a portrait of George Washington as she fled just before the British arrived. Congress's library, with roughly three thousand books, was destroyed.

By 1814, new officers had been appointed to replace aging veterans of the American Revolution. The Americans seemed to find their footing and won important victories in Baltimore, Maryland, and Plattsburgh, New York. Peace with Britain came at last with the Treaty of Ghent, and fifty years of hostilities between England and America were finally at an end.

Another battle was at an end, too: the one between Jeffersonian Republicans and Federalists, especially those in New England. At the Hartford Convention of 1814–15 in Connecticut, the Federalists once more talked of breaking away to form their own country. But when news of the meeting spread, public opinion turned strongly against the Federalists.

Plans for secession withered. No states were going to break away to form a monarchy with close ties to Great Britain. The United States would remain whole, independent, and democratic.

Dolley Madison, wife of James Madison, was one of the few women who were close to Jefferson while he was president.

※ ※

At home in Monticello, Jefferson was under siege from the public. Patsy once guessed that she had been asked to find beds for fifty overnight guests. The smashing of glass announced one visitor; she had jabbed her parasol through a window as she strained to catch a glimpse of Jefferson. Other strangers, hoping to see the writer of the Declaration of Independence, waited in the hall for Jefferson to walk from his study to the main part of the house for dinner.

After Jefferson's death, a writer working on a biography of him once walked the grounds of Monticello with Wormley Hughes, a former slave of Jefferson's. Pointing to the places for carriages under the North Terrace, the writer asked, "Wormley, how often were these filled, in Mr. Jefferson's time?"

"Every night, sir, in summer, and we commonly had two or three carriages under that tree," Hughes said.

"It took all hands to take care of your visitors?" the writer asked.

"Yes, sir, and the whole farm to feed them."

As he grew older, Jefferson had difficulty hearing different voices speaking at the same time, and he needed eyeglasses more often. Otherwise, he was in good health, suffering only from rare fevers. The headaches that had plagued him in times of stress seemed to vanish now that he was back home.

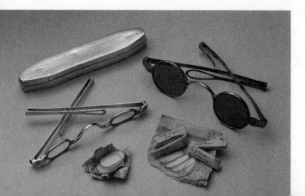

The optician John McAllister designed these eyeglasses specifically for Jefferson.

He fell ill in 1818 but recovered. In that same year, Abigail Adams died. Jefferson wrote warmly to John Adams, noting that words could do little in such an hour of grief, a lesson he had learned all too well. Still, he told Adams, he was "mingling sincerely my tears with yours."

Despite war, grief, and anxieties about the future, Jefferson was an optimist. "I think, with you, that it is a good world on the whole," he once wrote to John Adams. Adams was not so sure. "I dare not look beyond my nose" into the future, he wrote. "Our money, our commerce, our religion, our national and state constitutions, even our arts and sciences, are so many seedplots of division, faction, sedition, and rebellion."

Jefferson believed in the future, and why not? His own lifetime showed how far human beings could progress. The past, he thought, was not a perfect, magical time, always better than the present, whatever the present might be. "Some men . . . ascribe to the men of the preceding age a wisdom more than human," he wrote.

> *I knew that age well: I belonged to it, and labored with it. It deserved well of its country. It was very like the present, but without the experience of the present. . . . I know that laws and institutions must go hand in hand with the progress of the human mind. . . . We might as well require a man to wear still the coat which fitted him when a boy, a civilized society to remain ever under the regimen [rule] of their barbarous ancestors.*

He loved new ideas, new thoughts, new creations: "The fact is that one new idea leads to another, that to a third and so on through a course of time, until someone, with whom no one of these ideas is original, combines all together, and produces what is justly called a new invention." For Jefferson, the future was full of wonderful possibilities. "When I contemplate the immense advances in science, and discoveries in the arts which have been made within the period of my life, I look forward with confidence to equal advances by the present generation; and have no doubt they will consequently be as much wiser than we have been, as we than our fathers were," he wrote.

It was with the future in mind that Jefferson offered to sell Congress his own beloved library to replace the 3,000 books burned by the British in the War of 1812. Jefferson owned 6,487 books, which a newspaper called "beyond all price." Congress accepted his offer, and Jefferson's own library was the beginning of the new Library of Congress.

As the years passed, Jefferson turned more and more of his attention toward another project that he believed would make it possible for future generations to be wiser and better than those who came before. It was a university in Charlottesville. Jefferson meant the school to educate the statesmen, lawmakers, and judges who would manage the government once he and his generation were gone.

For him, nothing was more important than education. The power of government, he wrote, must come from the people

THE LIBRARY OF CONGRESS

The Library of Congress first took shape in 1800, when John Adams decided that lawmakers needed books to use for research. Five thousand dollars was budgeted for buying "such books as may be necessary for the use of Congress—and for putting up a suitable apartment for containing them," as he wrote.

When Congress decided to buy Thomas Jefferson's library to replace the three thousand books destroyed by the British in the War of 1812, the Library of Congress widened its scope. Now it contained more than books on law, history, and economics. Jefferson's personal library was also full of works on the arts, architecture, science, and philosophy. It was all useful, as far as Jefferson was concerned. He believed that members of Congress needed books of all kinds.

Since 1870, the Library of Congress has received two copies of every printed item that is copyrighted in the United States—not only books but pamphlets, maps, music recordings, prints, and photographs as well. On its shelves today there are more than 155 million items in 460 languages. They are kept in three separate buildings in Washington, D.C. The oldest of the three is the Thomas Jefferson Building.

A reading room in the Library of Congress in Washington, D.C.

who were governed; that was the only safe place for it. But those people must be sensible enough to manage that power. "If we think them not enlightened enough to exercise their control," he wrote, "the remedy is, not to take it from them" but to educate them. Wise and thoughtful citizens would be the safeguard of democracy in the years to come.

The making of the University of Virginia was Jefferson's last great effort of will and leadership. As with so much in his life, there were compromises and struggles. (He spent too much money, as he often did.) But in the end, Jefferson created something that endured.

The words of the Declaration of Independence lived on once Jefferson himself was gone. The country that began with thirteen states, and then was doubled by the purchase of the Louisiana Territory, lived on. Jefferson's ideas of a nation ruled by a strong president lived on. And so did the University of Virginia.

The University of Virginia was designed to give educational expression to Jefferson's devotion to the life of the mind and the pursuit of reason.

CHAPTER TWENTY-FOUR
The Wolf by the Ear

*From the Battle of Bunker's Hill to the Treaty of Paris
we never had so ominous a question.*
—Thomas Jefferson

On Friday, December 10, 1819, Jefferson took note of a debate in Congress that would shape the future of the country. The question was this: Should Missouri become the twenty-fourth state of the United States? And, if so, should slavery be legal there?

The House of Representatives voted to admit Missouri to the Union, but only as a free state. The Senate did not agree.

Ever since the Constitutional Convention, Northeastern-ers had worried that the slave-owning states of the South would gain too much power. They had a clear reason for this worry. The more people who lived in a state, the more representatives that state was allowed to send to Congress. Slaves were not allowed to vote, but they were counted as people—in a way. Each slave in a state was counted as three-fifths of a person. The more slaves who lived in a state, the more power that state had in Congress.

The free states feared that the slave states would use their numbers in Congress to turn votes to their own advantage. The slave-owning states feared that the free states wanted to make slavery illegal.

To Jefferson, it was the worst of hours. He knew that slavery was a moral wrong. He believed that it would, in time, be abolished. He could not bring himself, however, to work directly for the end of slavery. And he knew that the division between North and South over the issue could put the whole country in danger.

He was open with John Adams about his fears. "The Missouri question is a breaker on which we lose the Missouri country by revolt, and what more, God only knows," he wrote.

Jefferson was open to the idea of freeing all slaves—it "would not cost me a second thought," he claimed. It was the question of what was to be done with those slaves *after* they were freed that he could not settle in his own mind.

The only solution he could envision was to send freed slaves back to Africa or elsewhere. And this he could see no way to do. "Nothing is more certainly written in the book of fate than that these people are to be free. Nor is it less certain that two races, equally free, cannot live in the same government," he wrote.

Jefferson, however, did not come up with a solution. "As it is, we have the wolf by the ear, and we can neither hold him nor safely let him go," he worried. "Justice is in one scale, and self-preservation in the other."

Jefferson could not imagine a multiracial society, yet he saw one every day. Two races (though they were not equally free) lived in his household. His own children were part of that society; his white children and grandchildren grew up side by side with his biracial children, whom he kept enslaved.

How is it possible to explain the contradiction? Maybe Jefferson felt that if he were the one in control, he would be able to keep matters in hand. This had been his attitude about the country at large. He had been anxious about strong presidential powers until he was the one wielding those powers.

A twenty-foot excavation trench at Monticello's slave quarters, Mulberry Row, revealing remains of a previously undocumented building.

Then he was glad to expand the powers of the presidency by acquiring the Louisiana Territory or enforcing an embargo on what Americans could buy or sell.

Perhaps the role he played at Monticello—as father and grandfather, as slaveholder, as head of the household and owner of the plantation—made him think of his own home as an exception, a place where he could manage everything.

The debate in Congress was finally settled by a compromise. Missouri was admitted as a slave state. In the country as a whole, except in Missouri itself, slavery was to be allowed south of the parallel 36°30' north. Slaves who escaped from slave territory into free were to be caught and returned to their masters; anyone who helped them flee would be breaking the law.

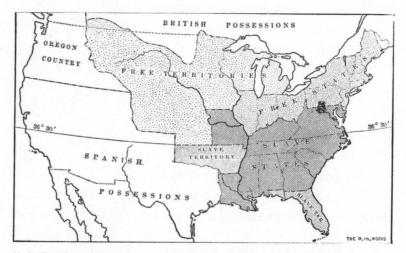

Under the Missouri Compromise, parallel 36°30' north divided the nation into slave states and free states. Slavery was forbidden within the Louisiana Purchase north of the 36th parallel and was allowed in the new state of Missouri and in states south of the 36th parallel.

In the end, Jefferson could see slavery only as a tragedy. He called it "a hideous blot," but it was not a blot he felt capable of erasing. The man who, all his life, found ways to gather and wield power—political power, power of the mind, power over his own family, power even over the kind of wine he served at his table and the kind of flowers he planted in his garden—chose to consider himself helpless when it came to slavery.

"There is nothing I would not sacrifice to a practicable plan" to ending slavery, he wrote in 1814, but this was not true. He was not willing to sacrifice his own way of life. Others were. Some wealthy Virginians recognized that the blight of slavery had to go, and they did what was within their power by freeing their own slaves. Other politicians were debating the issue of slavery, forcing white Americans everywhere to take notice. Jefferson chose not to take action.

He was wrong about slavery. As a practical politician, he simply did not see—or was not willing to see—a way to bring it to an end. He did what politicians often do and left the problem to those who would come after him. "I leave its accomplishment as the work of another generation," he wrote in 1825. "The abolition of the evil is not impossible. . . . Every plan should be adopted, every experiment tried, which may do something toward the ultimate object."

But he would not undertake these experiments himself. When it came to slavery, Jefferson, always curious and eager to explore new ideas, did what he almost never did: he gave up.

He gave up when it came to money as well. Jefferson was in debt for much of his life. Planters of his time and place often were. They owned valuable lands, houses, and slaves but frequently had little cash. So they borrowed. Jefferson did the same—and so had his father. Along with his plantation, Jefferson had inherited his father's debt. He tried to pay it off but never entirely succeeded. As his life went on, he borrowed more money whenever he needed it—and he needed it often.

Why did Jefferson, who sought power over people and events, take so little control over his own finances? Part of the explanation may lie in his tendency to avoid conflict, to make the easy choice. It was easier to pay off old debts by contracting new ones than to face the difficulties of the moment.

And perhaps his sense of his own power made him less concerned about his debts than he should have been. The prospect of ruin—running out of money completely, losing his home and lands and slaves—may never have seemed real to him. And so he took on more and more debt, bought presents for his grandchildren with borrowed money, and signed notes for friends and family, promising to pay off their debts if they could not. The man who loved power was sacrificing his own power and his family's future. As with slavery, when it came to money, Jefferson's ability to think one way and live another was remarkable.

❧ ❧

Arriving at Monticello in a procession of trumpets and banners, the Marquis de Lafayette stepped out of his carriage on a brilliant autumn day in November 1824. Lafayette, now sixty-seven years old, had come to Monticello as part of a farewell tour of America.

Stooped with age at eighty-one, Jefferson walked toward his guest. They embraced, two old revolutionaries who had seen the best and worst of their times and of their countries.

"My dear Jefferson!" said the guest.

"My dear Lafayette!" replied the host.

They had not laid eyes on each other for thirty years, and Jefferson was determined to honor Lafayette's service to the United States. At a banquet in Lafayette's honor in Charlottesville, Jefferson drafted a toast to be read.

His deeds in the war of independence you have heard and read. They are known to you. . . . His deeds in the peace which followed that war are perhaps not known to you; but I can attest them. When I was stationed in his country . . . he made our cause his own. . . . Honor him, then, as your benefactor in peace, as well as in war.

Jefferson's toast had a broader message to his countrymen, most of them now much younger than he was.

Portrait of the Marquis de Lafayette.

*Born and bred among your fathers . . . I labored in fellow-
ship with them through that arduous [difficult] struggle
which, freeing us from foreign bondage, established us in
the rights of self-government; rights which had blessed
ourselves, and will bless . . . all the nations of the earth.*

In old age, Jefferson was the Jefferson of his youth, a man
who honored the work of politics, the comradeship of service, and the ideas that drove flawed men to fight for causes
larger than themselves.

Jefferson always had in mind what would bring the
United States and the world to freedom, peace, and happiness.
He also had his thoughts about what individual human beings could do to reach that state. When he was asked to send
advice to a young man, he settled down to write a long letter.
It was a subject that had always interested him: how to live a
virtuous life.

"Adore God," he wrote. "Reverence [respect] and cherish
your parents. Love your neighbor as yourself, and your country more than yourself. Be just. Be true. Murmur not [do not
protest] at the ways of Providence."

There was more.

1. *Never put off till tomorrow what you can do today.*
2. *Never trouble another for what you can do yourself.*
3. *Never spend your money before you have it.*
4. *Never buy what you do not want, because it is cheap;
   it will be dear [expensive] to you.*
5. *Pride costs us more than hunger, thirst, and cold.*

6. *We never repent of having eaten too little.*
7. *Nothing is troublesome that we do willingly.*
8. *How much pain have cost us [How much do we suffer from] the evils which have never happened.*
9. *Take things always by their smooth handle. [Look for the easiest way to do things.]*
10. *When angry, count ten before you speak; if very angry, a hundred.*

Jefferson's health had slowly been declining. He tried to keep his independence, but it was harder and harder for him to do the things he had always done. One day toward the end of 1822, he put a foot wrong, and a terrace at Monticello gave way under his weight. He fell, struck the ground, and broke his left arm. It healed, but other accidents awaited. In May 1823, he was on his usual ride when he fell off his horse as it was crossing a river. He came close to drowning before he got to a shallow place where he could struggle to his feet. His family demanded that he give up riding by himself; he refused.

But old age caught up with him at last. When the fiftieth anniversary of the Declaration of Independence came near, he was too ill to travel to Washington for a celebration. Instead, he drafted a letter. "All eyes are opened, or are opening, to the rights of man," he wrote. "The mass of mankind has not been born with saddles on their backs, nor a favored few booted and spurred, ready to ride them. . . . These are grounds of hope for others. For ourselves, let the annual return of this day forever refresh our recollections of these rights, and an undiminished devotion to them."

These were his words of farewell to the nation that he had helped to found and had led through so much. His farewell to James Madison was more personal. "Take care of me when dead," Jefferson wrote in a letter to his old friend.

Soon Jefferson was forced to stay in bed. He continued to read, but his illness grew worse as the last days of June approached.

The end was at hand.

Close-up of the signatures on the Declaration of Independence.

CHAPTER TWENTY-FIVE

No, Doctor, Nothing More

The loss of Mr. Jefferson is one over which the whole world will mourn.
—DABNEY CARR JR., NEPHEW OF THOMAS JEFFERSON

On Saturday, June 24, 1826, Jefferson painfully put pen to paper to ask Robley Dunglison to visit him. The doctor left as soon as he got the note. When he arrived, he found that Jefferson had forced himself to rise from bed and walk into the parlor, as though to greet the doctor in the old ordinary way.

Dunglison put him back into bed. The doctor was worried

Portrait of Thomas Jefferson Randolph, Jefferson's eldest grandson.

that "the attack would prove fatal. Nor did Mr. Jefferson indulge in any other opinion," he remembered. Jefferson knew that this was the end.

But Thomas Jefferson put all of his will toward one last goal: he wanted to survive until the Fourth of July.

As he lay dying, his daughter sat with him during the day. A grandson, Thomas Jefferson Randolph, and Nicholas Trist, who had married one of his granddaughters, kept watch with him in the nights. "His mind was always clear—it never wandered," Randolph said. "He conversed freely and gave directions as to his private affairs."

Jefferson told his grandson what he wanted done about his coffin and burial. There was to be nothing showy or grand. He wanted a simple church service for his funeral, and he asked to be laid to rest on the western slope of Monticello, where he had buried Dabney Carr so many decades before— and then his mother, and then his wife.

Jefferson's rooms, ordinarily so private, filled as his strength faded. He said good-bye to his family one by one, speaking to each of them in turn. He smiled at an eight-year-old grandson and said, "George does not understand what all this means." He quoted the Gospel of Luke to a great-granddaughter, saying, "Lord, now lettest thou thy servant depart in peace."

For Patsy, his only surviving daughter, he composed a poem, which he enclosed in a little box that she did not open until after he had died. "Then farewell, my dear, my lov'd daughter, adieu! / The last pang of life is parting from you," he wrote for her.

Lying in bed, Jefferson told stories of the Revolution. He kept close track of time, willing himself to live to see, however dimly, the fiftieth anniversary of the Declaration of Independence.

On the evening of July 3, at about seven o'clock, Jefferson spoke. "Ah! Doctor, are you still there?" he asked Dunglison. "Is it the Fourth?"

Portrait of Martha (Patsy) Washington Jefferson, Jefferson's daughter.

"It soon will be," Dunglison answered.

Jefferson swallowed some laudanum, medicine to ease his pain. Two hours later, Dunglison woke him for another dose.

"No, Doctor, nothing more," Jefferson said.

The hours passed with agonizing slowness. Late, but before midnight had come, Jefferson awoke. Again he asked, "This is the Fourth?" Nicholas Trist, watching by his bed, did not answer. Jefferson would not be put off. "This is the Fourth?" he repeated.

Trist could not bear to disappoint Jefferson. He nodded.

"Ah," said Jefferson, "just as I wished."

Perhaps he knew, somehow, that it was not true, that the

anniversary of the declaration had not yet come. He fought on, breathing still.

At last, the clock above his bed chimed twelve times. It was the Fourth of July.

Drifting in and out of sleep, Jefferson appeared to be dreaming. He murmured about the Revolutionary Committee of Safety and gestured as if he were writing. "Warn the Committee to be on the alert," he said. In his last hours, he was still struggling to defend the American cause, even if the dangers were only in his imagination.

At four o'clock in the morning, Jefferson gave some directions to his slaves. These were the last words he spoke. At ten minutes before one o'clock in the afternoon on Tuesday, July 4, 1826, Thomas Jefferson died in his bed, three miles from the place where he had been born, more than eighty years before, as a subject of the British Empire.

"To me he has been more than a father, and I have ever loved and reverenced him with my whole heart," his nephew Dabney Carr Jr. wrote a week later. James Madison wrote, "He lives and will live in the memory and gratitude of the wise and the good . . . as a benefactor of humankind."

Jefferson's memorandum on his grave and epitaph emphasized his Enlightenment achievements rather than his political achievements. He is noted as the author of the Declaration of Independence and the Virginia bill of religious liberty, as well as the founder of the University of Virginia. The offices he held, however, are not mentioned.

The promise that Jefferson had made in Paris was honored. He kept his word to Sally Hemings. Her children were free.

Two of the children of Thomas Jefferson and Sally Hemings, Beverly and Harriet, had been allowed to leave Monticello in the early 1820s. Both are said to have lived as whites. According to their brother Madison Hemings, "Harriet married a white man in good standing in Washington City. . . . She raised a family of children, and so far as I knew they were never suspected of being tainted with African blood in the community where she lived or lives." Madison himself was freed by Jefferson's will and moved to Ohio, as did his brother Eston. After a time, Eston settled in Wisconsin, changed his name to Eston Jefferson, and declared himself to be white.

In his will, Jefferson also freed three other members of the Hemings family: Burwell Colbert, John Hemings, and Joe Fosset. He freed no other slaves—only Hemingses.

Sally Hemings herself, now fifty-three years old, soon moved to Charlottesville and lived there as a free woman. Jefferson did not name her in his will, but he may have made his wishes clear to Patsy and his heirs. In 1834, Patsy gave Sally Hemings "her time"—an unofficial way to set her free. She never lived as a slave again.

Sally died in 1835. She left some mementos of Jefferson to her children—a pair of his glasses, an inkwell, and a shoe buckle.

When he died, Thomas Jefferson's home, land, and remaining slaves were sold to pay his debts. His ideas and his public work lasted after him. His personal world did not.

EXECUTOR'S SALE.

Will be sold, on the fifteenth of January, at Monticello, in the county of Albemarle, the whole of the residue of the personal estate of Thomas Jefferson, dec., consisting of **130 VALUABLE NEGROES,** Stock, Crop, &c. Household and Kitchen Furniture. The attention of the public is earnestly invited to this property. The negroes are believed to be the most valuable for their number ever offered at one time in the State of Virginia. The household furniture, many valuable historical and portrait paintings, busts of marble and plaister of distinguished individuals; one of marble of Thomas Jefferson, by Caracci, with the pedestal and truncated column on which it stands; a polygraph or copying instrument used by Thomas Jefferson, for the last twenty-five years; with various other articles curious and useful to men of business and private families. The terms of sale will be accommodating and made known previous to the day. The sale will be continued from day to day until completed. This sale being unavoidable, it is a sufficient guarantee to the public, that it will take place at the time and place appointed.

THOMAS J. RANDOLPH,
Executor of Th: Jefferson, dec.
January 6, 1827—2t

The paintings and busts of Thos. Jefferson, dec. will not be offered for sale on the 15th of January next; but will be sent to some one of the large cities and then sold, after due notice.

BY AUTHORITY OF CONGRESS

Because of overwhelming debts, Jefferson's heirs could not save Monticello in the wake of his death in 1826.

Six hundred miles away, John Adams, ninety years old, died on the same day as Thomas Jefferson. His final words were said to be about his old friend and rival: "Thomas Jefferson survives."

And so he does.

All Honor to Jefferson

Jefferson's principles are sources of light. . . . They burn with the fervor of the heart.
— WOODROW WILSON, PRESIDENT OF THE UNITED STATES

"If Jefferson was wrong, America is wrong," wrote a biographer in 1874. "If America is right, Jefferson was right."

That is a remarkable burden to put on any one man or any one vision of politics. But the observation rings true. The issues that consumed Jefferson still consume us today: liberty and power, rights and responsibilities, the keeping of peace and the waging of war.

Had he been only a philosopher, he would not have endured as he has. Had he been only a lawmaker, or only a diplomat, or only an inventor, or only an author, or only an educator, or only a president, he would not have endured as he has.

Jefferson still means so much to us today because we can see in him all the wondrous possibilities of the human experience. We can see his thirst for knowledge, his ability to create, his love of family and of friends, his hunger to do great things, his longing for applause and praise, his gathering of power, his way of bending the world to his own vision.

So who was he, really? The real Jefferson was like so many of us: a bundle of contradictions, flaws, sins, and virtues that can never be neatly smoothed into a tidy whole. The one thing that was constant in his life was his need for power and control. In his country, in his government, in his home and family, he shaped what was around him to suit his ideas of how everything should be.

His brilliance and accomplishments will always be remembered. Yet because of his flaws and his failures, we see that he is human, too. He achieved great things, but he also gave in to temptation and made compromises. He was not all he could have been. But no politician—no human being—ever is.

Despite all his shortcomings and disappointments and mistakes, he left America and the world better than they had been before he entered politics and took his place in his country's history.

Jefferson never gave up on America. In many ways, he brought the country into being, and he watched over it in its early years with anxious care. "And I have observed this march of civilization advancing from the sea coast, passing over us like a cloud of light, increasing our knowledge and improving our condition," he wrote in 1824, "and where this progress will stop no one can say."

The Jefferson Memorial in Washington, D.C., opened in 1943.

IN JEFFERSON'S WORLD

THOMAS JEFFERSON'S FAMILY

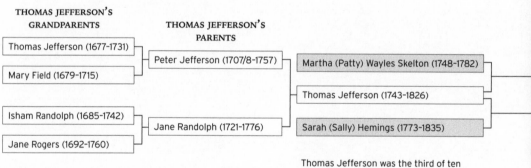

THOMAS JEFFERSON'S GRANDPARENTS

Thomas Jefferson (1677-1731)

Mary Field (1679-1715)

Isham Randolph (1685-1742)

Jane Rogers (1692-1760)

THOMAS JEFFERSON'S PARENTS

Peter Jefferson (1707/8-1757)

Jane Randolph (1721-1776)

Martha (Patty) Wayles Skelton (1748-1782)

Thomas Jefferson (1743-1826)

Sarah (Sally) Hemings (1773-1835)

Thomas Jefferson was the third of ten children born to Peter Jefferson and Jane Randolph.

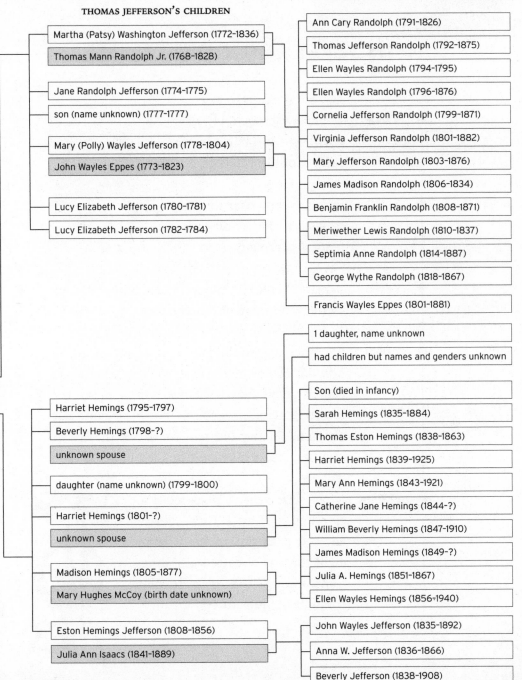

THOMAS JEFFERSON'S CHILDREN

THOMAS JEFFERSON'S GRANDCHILDREN

Martha (Patsy) Washington Jefferson (1772-1836)
Thomas Mann Randolph Jr. (1768-1828)

Jane Randolph Jefferson (1774-1775)
son (name unknown) (1777-1777)

Mary (Polly) Wayles Jefferson (1778-1804)
John Wayles Eppes (1773-1823)

Lucy Elizabeth Jefferson (1780-1781)
Lucy Elizabeth Jefferson (1782-1784)

Ann Cary Randolph (1791-1826)
Thomas Jefferson Randolph (1792-1875)
Ellen Wayles Randolph (1794-1795)
Ellen Wayles Randolph (1796-1876)
Cornelia Jefferson Randolph (1799-1871)
Virginia Jefferson Randolph (1801-1882)
Mary Jefferson Randolph (1803-1876)
James Madison Randolph (1806-1834)
Benjamin Franklin Randolph (1808-1871)
Meriwether Lewis Randolph (1810-1837)
Septimia Anne Randolph (1814-1887)
George Wythe Randolph (1818-1867)

Francis Wayles Eppes (1801-1881)

1 daughter, name unknown
had children but names and genders unknown

Harriet Hemings (1795-1797)
Beverly Hemings (1798-?)
unknown spouse

daughter (name unknown) (1799-1800)

Harriet Hemings (1801-?)
unknown spouse

Madison Hemings (1805-1877)
Mary Hughes McCoy (birth date unknown)

Eston Hemings Jefferson (1808-1856)
Julia Ann Isaacs (1841-1889)

Son (died in infancy)
Sarah Hemings (1835-1884)
Thomas Eston Hemings (1838-1863)
Harriet Hemings (1839-1925)
Mary Ann Hemings (1843-1921)
Catherine Jane Hemings (1844-?)
William Beverly Hemings (1847-1910)
James Madison Hemings (1849-?)
Julia A. Hemings (1851-1867)
Ellen Wayles Hemings (1856-1940)

John Wayles Jefferson (1835-1892)
Anna W. Jefferson (1836-1866)
Beverly Jefferson (1838-1908)

IN JEFFERSON'S LIFETIME

1743 Thomas Jefferson was born in Virginia as a subject of King George II.

Johann Sebastian Bach.

1750 Baroque composer Johann Sebastian Bach died in Leipzig, Germany.

1752 Benjamin Franklin experimented with lightning by flying a kite in a thunderstorm.

1758 A comet appeared, precisely as predicted by Edmond Halley, astronomer and mathematician. Halley calculated the comet's orbit using the laws of gravity as worked out by his friend Isaac Newton. (Halley did not live to see the comet that now bears his name; he died in 1742.)

1760s James Hargreaves invented the spinning jenny. This device allowed a single worker to spin eight threads of cotton at a time, transforming the way textiles could be manufactured.

A spinning jenny.

1762 Catherine the Great became empress of the Russian Empire. Her reign is known as Russia's golden age.

1763 King George III of England issued the proclamation of 1763, which promised that land between the Appalachian Mountains and the Mississippi River, from the Great Lakes to north of the Floridas, would be reserved for Native American tribes. Europeans were forbidden to settle there.

1765 Great Britain passed the Stamp Act to tax its American colonies.

1769 James Watt patented a much-improved steam engine. This invention would impact machine productivity and travel.

James Watt.

1769–1770 The great famine of Bengal killed millions of people in what are the present-day Indian states of Bengal and Bihar.

1770 Five American colonists were shot by British troops in what was called the Boston Massacre.

1771 The first edition of the *Encyclopædia Britannica* was completed. The reference work took up three volumes.

1773 During the Boston Tea Party, American colonists threw 342 chests of tea into Boston Harbor.

1774 Great Britain imposed the Coercive Acts, or the Intolerable Acts, on its North American colonies.

The East India Company (which owned the tea dumped in Boston Harbor) appointed its first governor-general of India.

1776 Thomas Paine published *Common Sense,* and Thomas Jefferson wrote the Declaration of Independence.

The economist Adam Smith published *The Wealth of Nations,* one of the first written accounts to explain the connections between politics and economics.

1778 Captain James Cook and his men became the first Europeans to see the Hawaiian Islands.

Statue of Adam Smith.

1779   Thomas Jefferson became governor of Virginia.

1783   The American Revolution was formally ended.

In Versailles, France, brothers Joseph-Michel and Jacques-Étienne Montgolfier experimented with an early hot-air balloon, sending a sheep, a rooster, and a duck aloft.

Hot-air balloon designed by the Montgolfier brothers.

Simón Bolívar was born in Venezuela. As an adult he helped free what are now Bolivia, Panama, Colombia, Ecuador, and Venezuela from Spanish colonial rule.

1784   Thomas Jefferson arrived in Paris.

The Second Treaty of Fort Stanwix effectively put an end to the Iroquois Federation, a powerful alliance of the Mohawk, Oneida, Onondaga, Cayuga, Seneca, and Tuscarora tribes. The alliance was split, with three tribes remaining in New York, two withdrawing to Canada, and one later moving to Wisconsin.

The first white settlement in Alaska was established on Kodiak Island by a Russian merchant, Grigory Shelikhov.

1787   British politician William Wilberforce helped to found the Society for Effecting the Abolition of the Slave Trade.

The first former slaves settled in the African nation of Sierra Leone.

1788   The first ships filled with convicts sentenced to transportation from England arrived in Botany Bay, Australia.

1789   The Bastille, a Paris prison, was stormed by a rioting crowd.

1791   Slaves on the French colony Saint-Domingue rose in rebellion. Saint-Domingue became an independent nation, known as Haiti, thirteen years later.

1792   Mary Wollstonecraft published *A Vindication of the Rights of Woman*.

Mary Wollstonecraft.

1793   Louis XVI and Marie Antoinette, king and queen of France, were executed.

1800   The United States government met in Washington, D.C., for the first time.

1801   Thomas Jefferson was inaugurated as president of the United States.

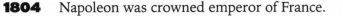

1804 Napoleon was crowned emperor of France.

1805 Lewis and Clark reached the Pacific Ocean.

1809 Abraham Lincoln was born in Kentucky.

1810 One of the most successful and feared pirates in history, Ching Shih, or Zheng Yi Sao ("wife of Cheng"), accepted amnesty from the Chinese government. She retired peacefully.

1813 The Shawnee chief Tecumseh, a leader of resistance to white settlement in Native American lands, was killed in battle.

1820 The Missouri Compromise allowed Missouri, a slave state, to enter the Union as the twenty-fourth state. The compromise prohibited slavery north of the 36°30' parallel, except within Missouri.

1825 Charles Darwin, at age sixteen, arrived at Edinburgh University to study medicine.

The Japanese government issued the Order to Drive Away Foreign Ships, which included instructions to arrest or kill any non-Japanese who set foot in Japan.

1826 Thomas Jefferson died.

TIMELINE:
Thomas Jefferson and the American Revolution

TIMELINE OF THE REVOLUTIONARY WAR AND EARLY AMERICAN HISTORY	YEAR	TIMELINE OF THOMAS JEFFERSON'S LIFE
	1743	Jefferson born at Shadwell Plantation, in Virginia.
	1757	Peter Jefferson (Jefferson's father) died.
	1760–62	Jefferson attended the College of William and Mary.
	1762	Jefferson began to study law with George Wythe.
French and Indian War, or Seven Years' War, ended.	1763	
Sugar Act passed.	1764	
Stamp Act passed.	1765	
Townshend Revenue Act passed.	1767	
	1769	Jefferson elected to the Virginia House of Burgesses.

Timeline of the Revolutionary War and Early American History	Year	Timeline of Thomas Jefferson's Life
Five American colonists killed by British troops during the Boston Massacre.	1770	
	1772	Jefferson married Martha (Patty) Wayles Skelton. Daughter Martha (Patsy) Washington Jefferson born.
Boston Tea Party	1773	Jefferson's father-in-law, John Wayles, died. The Jeffersons inherited several slaves, including Elizabeth and Sally Hemings.
Coercive Acts (or Intolerable Acts) passed. First Continental Congress	1774	Jefferson wrote *A Summary View of the Rights of British America*. Daughter Jane Randolph Jefferson born.
Patrick Henry made "Give me liberty or give me death" speech. Jefferson was in the crowd to hear him. Revolutionary War began. Battles of Lexington and Concord. Second Continental Congress. George Washington named commander in chief of Continental army. Battle of Bunker Hill	1775	Jefferson elected to Second Continental Congress. Jefferson, with John Dickinson, wrote *A Declaration of the Causes and Necessity for Taking Up Arms*. Daughter Jane Randolph Jefferson died.

Timeline of the Revolutionary War and Early American History	Year	Timeline of Thomas Jefferson's Life
Declaration of Independence adopted by Congress. British occupied New York City. George Washington led his troops across Delaware River and defeated German troops (fighting for the British) at Trenton, NJ.	1776	Jefferson wrote the Declaration of Independence. Jane Randolph Jefferson (Thomas Jefferson's mother) died.
Washington's troops won second victory at Princeton, NJ. Americans defeated British at Saratoga, NY. Continental army camped for the winter at Valley Forge, PA. The first constitution, known as the Articles of Confederation, was written by a thirteen-member committee of the Second Continental Congress.	1777	Jefferson drafted bill for Virginia Statute for Religious Freedom. Unnamed son with Martha (Patty) born and died.
France entered the war on the American side. British occupied Savannah, GA.	1778	Daughter Mary (Polly) Wayles Jefferson born.
John Paul Jones, captain of the *Bonhomme Richard*, captured the British man-of-war *Serapis*.	1779	Jefferson began first term as governor of Virginia.

Timeline of the Revolutionary War and Early American History	Year	Timeline of Thomas Jefferson's Life
British captured Charleston, SC. British forces under Benedict Arnold invaded Virginia.	1780	Jefferson began second term as governor of Virginia. Daughter Lucy Elizabeth Jefferson born.
General Cornwallis surrendered to General George Washington at Yorktown, VA.	1781	British captured Richmond, VA, and attempted to arrest Jefferson, who fled the city. British troops arrived at Monticello and attempted to arrest Jefferson a second time. Jefferson's second term as governor of Virginia ended. Daughter Lucy Elizabeth Jefferson died.
	1782	Lucy Elizabeth Jefferson (Jefferson's second daughter with the name) born. Wife Martha (Patty) died. First house on site of Monticello completed.
Treaty of Paris formally ended the Revolutionary War.	1783	Jefferson elected to Congress.
	1784	Jefferson sent to France to represent American interests. Daughter Lucy Elizabeth Jefferson died.

Timeline of the Revolutionary War and Early American History	Year	Timeline of Thomas Jefferson's Life
Constitutional Convention created second constitution for the United States.	1787	Polly Jefferson and Sally Hemings arrived in France.
George Washington elected to become the first president.	1788	
	1789	Jefferson returned from France.
	1790	Jefferson began service as secretary of state under George Washington.
	1793	Jefferson resigned as secretary of state.
	1795	Daughter Harriet Hemings born.
	1796	Remodeling of Monticello began.
John Adams became president of the United States.	1797	Jefferson began service as vice president. Daughter Harriet Hemings died.
	1798	Son William Beverly Hemings born.
George Washington died.	1799	Unnamed daughter with Sally Hemings born. She died a short time later.
John Adams moved into the President's House.	1800	

TIMELINE OF THE REVOLUTIONARY WAR AND EARLY AMERICAN HISTORY	YEAR	TIMELINE OF THOMAS JEFFERSON'S LIFE
	1801	Jefferson ended term as vice president and began first term as president of the United States. Harriet Hemings (Jefferson's second daughter with the name) born.
	1802	James Callender made Jefferson's relationship with Sally Hemings public.
	1803	Louisiana Purchase completed. The Corps of Discovery organized. Lewis and Clark set out on expedition the following year (1804).
Aaron Burr, vice president of the United States, killed Alexander Hamilton.	1804	Daughter Mary (Polly) Wayles Jefferson died.
	1805	Lewis and Clark expedition arrived at the Pacific Ocean. Son Madison Hemings born.
	1806	Lewis and Clark expedition returned home.
	1807	Jefferson signed embargo bill, forbidding trade with foreign nations.
	1808	Son Eston Hemings Jefferson born.

TIMELINE OF THE REVOLUTIONARY WAR AND EARLY AMERICAN HISTORY	YEAR	TIMELINE OF THOMAS JEFFERSON'S LIFE
James Madison became president of the United States.	1809	Jefferson retired from the presidency. Remodeling at Monticello completed.
War of 1812 began.	1812	Jefferson began exchanging letters once more with John Adams.
War of 1812 ended.	1815	
James Monroe became president of the United States.	1817	
Missouri Compromise allowed Missouri to enter the Union and divided the territory of the Louisiana Purchase into areas open and closed to slavery.	1820	
	1824	Final meeting of Jefferson and the Marquis de Lafayette.
John Quincy Adams became president of the United States.	1825	University of Virginia opened.
	1826	Jefferson died at Monticello.

WHO'S WHO

Abigail Adams first lady of the United States; married to John Adams. She and Thomas Jefferson were close friends, but driven apart by political differences.

John Adams lawyer; vice president and president of the United States; married to Abigail Adams. At times a friend, ally, and bitter political foe of Thomas Jefferson.

Norborne Berkeley, Lord Botetourt royal governor of the colony of Virginia.

Napoleon Bonaparte emperor of France.

Aaron Burr vice president of the United States during Thomas Jefferson's presidency; killed Alexander Hamilton in a duel in 1804; tried and acquitted for treason in 1807.

Napoleon Bonaparte.

Dabney Carr Thomas Jefferson's close friend and brother-in-law; married to Martha Jefferson.

William Clark army officer; coleader with Meriwether Lewis of the Corps of Discovery.

Francis Fauquier royal governor of the colony of Virginia.

George III king of Great Britain.

Alexander Hamilton lawyer; secretary of the Treasury under George Washington; lifelong political foe of Thomas Jefferson; killed in a duel by Aaron Burr.

Elizabeth Hemings slave owned by John Wayles and Thomas Jefferson; mother of Sally Hemings.

Sally Hemings slave owned by John Wayles and Thomas Jefferson; mother of Beverly, Harriet, Madison, and Eston Hemings.

Patrick Henry lawyer; politician; public speaker; member of the Virginia House of Burgesses; first governor of Virginia.

Jane Jefferson Thomas Jefferson's oldest sister.

Jane Randolph Jefferson mother of Thomas Jefferson; married to Peter Jefferson.

Martha (Patsy) Washington Jefferson daughter of Thomas and Patsy Jefferson; married Thomas Mann Randolph Jr.

Martha (Patty) Wayles Skelton Jefferson wife of Thomas Jefferson.

Mary (Polly) Wayles Jefferson daughter of Thomas and Patsy Jefferson; married John Wayles Eppes.

Peter Jefferson planter and surveyor; father of Thomas Jefferson; married to Jane Randolph.

Thomas Jefferson lawyer; governor of Virginia; U.S. minister to France; secretary of state; vice president and president of the United States; author of the Declaration of Independence; married to Martha (Patty) Jefferson.

Marquis de Lafayette (Marie-Joseph Paul Yves Roch Gilbert du Motier) military officer; supporter of the colonists in the Revolutionary War; one of the primary drafters of the Declaration of the Rights of Man and of the Citizen; close friend of Jefferson's during Jefferson's Paris years.

Meriwether Lewis military officer; personal secretary to Thomas Jefferson; coleader with William Clark of the Corps of Discovery.

Dolley Payne Madison first lady of the United States; married to James Madison.

James Madison secretary of state under Thomas Jefferson; fourth president of the United States; married to Dolley Madison; close friend, advisor, and political ally of Thomas Jefferson.

James Monroe negotiator of the Louisiana Purchase; fifth president of the United States; trusted political ally of Thomas Jefferson.

John Murray, Lord Dunmore last royal governor of Virginia.

Peyton Randolph lawyer; speaker of the Virginia House of Burgesses; cousin and mentor of Thomas Jefferson.

Thomas Mann Randolph Jr. member of Congress; governor of Virginia; married to Patsy Jefferson.

William Small professor at the College of William and Mary; taught Thomas Jefferson science, mathematics, and ethics.

George Washington commander in chief of the colonial armed forces; first president of the United States.

John Wayles lawyer; debt collector; slave trader; planter; father of Martha (Patty) Jefferson and Sally Hemings.

George Wythe lawyer; taught law to Thomas Jefferson.

Statue of George Washington.

REVOLUTIONARY WAR TIMES

- Crispus Attucks, a former slave of African and Native American descent who had escaped and was living as a free man in Massachusetts, was the first to die in the American Revolution. He was shot and killed in the Boston Massacre of 1770, a fight between British troops and colonists on the streets of Boston.

- The bell in the Pennsylvania State House (now Independence Hall) was called the Liberty Bell because of its engraved message: PROCLAIM LIBERTY THROUGHOUT ALL THE LAND UNTO ALL THE INHABITANTS THEREOF (Leviticus 25:10). The 2,080-pound bell, made mostly of copper and tin, was rung to announce the signing of the Declaration of Independence.

The Liberty Bell.

- Slavery was legal in all thirteen colonies at the time of the Revolutionary War. Roughly 20 percent of the people living in the colonies were black, and most, though not all, were enslaved.

- During the Revolutionary War, the Americans had two kinds of troops. The state militias could be called out by governors to deal with threats; they returned to their homes once the danger was past. The Continental army (the "Continentals"), commanded by George Washington, was made up of soldiers who enlisted for a certain amount of time and remained ready to fight for that period. They were better equipped and trained than the militias.

- In 1775, on his way to Concord, Massachusetts, to warn the colonists that British troops were on the march, Paul Revere was joined by two other riders, William Dawes and Samuel Prescott. All three were arrested by a British patrol. It was Prescott who escaped and carried the message on to Concord, where American militiamen gathered to fight.

- It's often said that Betsy Ross sewed the first American flag, but no one knows for sure.

- The colonial militia had special units, nicknamed minutemen because they were required to keep their guns and equipment with them at all times and be ready to fight in a single minute.

The Betsy Ross House in Philadelphia.

- A "doodle" was slang for a fool or a simpleton. British troops often sang a song called "Yankee Doodle" to mock the American colonists. But the colonists claimed the song as their own and made up dozens of new verses making fun of the British and boasting about their own side.

- The first battle of the Revolutionary War was fought on the town green of Lexington, Massachusetts, where a small band of militiamen faced hundreds of British troops. Eight Americans were killed before the militia retreated.

- Not every soldier or militiaman who fought in the Revolutionary War chose to do so. Some volunteered; others were drafted. Men who were drafted could find a substitute to fight for them or pay a fine of twenty pounds for the privilege of staying home.

- If you were a soldier in the Continental army, you would probably carry a musket, a cartridge box with twenty to thirty rounds of ammunition, a bayonet, and a pack for food with an iron fork, a spoon made of pewter or horn, a knife, a plate, and a cup, plus a canteen for water.

An example of the musket and canteen that a soldier in the Continental army might carry.

- It was not only native-born Americans who fought against the British. Baron von Steuben from Prussia, Thaddeus Kosciuszko and Casimir Pulaski, both from Poland, and the Marquis de Lafayette and the Comte de Rochambeau, both from France, were all crucial to the success of the Continental army.

- It was difficult (sometimes impossible) for the brand-new American government to find enough money to pay, feed, clothe, and arm its soldiers. In 1777, when camped for the winter at Valley Forge, Pennsylvania, Private Joseph Martin begged two fellow soldiers for a drink from their canteens (he finally paid them threepence for one swallow) and cooked the only food he could find—a small pumpkin—on a rock.

- Blacks also served during the Revolutionary War, on both the American and the British sides. In the South, approximately one thousand blacks were enlisted by the British army (who numbered sixty thousand, including foreign soldiers). They were promised their freedom for

Jean Baptiste Antoine de Verger's painting *Soldiers in Uniform* portrays a black soldier of the 1st Rhode Island Regiment, a New England militiaman, a frontier rifleman, and a French officer.

service and rarely saw combat. At least five thousand blacks fought for the Americans, serving as soldiers, cooks, and seamen.

- Not every colonist was a supporter of independence. About a fifth of colonists remained loyal to Great Britain. (Thomas Jefferson's cousin John Randolph was among them.) After the war, roughly a hundred thousand loyalists fled the country.

A set of George Washington's false teeth.

- Did you ever hear that George Washington had false teeth made of wood? Not true! Washington did indeed have dental trouble; by the time he was inaugurated as president, he had only a single tooth left. He had several sets of false teeth. Some were of ivory; some used human or animal teeth. But none were made of wood.

- The British troops were called redcoats for their bright-red uniforms. But George Washington's men often had to make do with whatever uniforms they could find. In 1776 Washington asked the government to provide each soldier with a "hunting shirt," a loose linen shirt common on the frontier. The shirts were cheap and practical, he wrote, and they had one additional advantage—they scared the enemy, "who think every such person [wearing a hunting shirt] is a complete marksman."

- During the American Revolution, women served mainly as cooks, nurses, maids, laundresses, seamstresses, water carriers, and sometimes spies. They were not allowed to join the military. Occasionally women saw combat. During the Battle of Monmouth in 1778, Mary Ludwig Hays McCauley accompanied her husband to the battlefield. She helped carry pitchers of water for cooling the cannons and the soldiers—hence her nickname, Molly Pitcher. When her husband was wounded, it is believed that Mary took his place behind the cannon. In 1781 Deborah Sampson, from Plympton, Massachusetts, fought for a year disguised as Robert Shurtleff before her identity was uncovered.

Molly Pitcher, the heroine of Monmouth.

- The fighting ended in 1781 when British general Charles Lord Cornwallis surrendered to the American and French forces in Yorktown, Virginia. Cornwallis sent his second-in-command to give his sword to the French commander in a formal gesture of surrender. But the Frenchman insisted that the sword be handed to George Washington. (Washington then directed his own second-in-command to take his enemy's sword.)

- As Cornwallis surrendered to the Continental army, the British band played a tune called "The World Turned Upside Down." The song captured the feelings of many who saw one of the world's largest and best-equipped military forces overturned by rebellious colonists.

WRITINGS

Thomas Jefferson is most famous for writing the Declaration of Independence. But it was not the only thing he wrote. Letters, reports, recipes, books in which he kept careful notes about his farms and gardens—Jefferson was always writing. He recorded the temperature of the day, his daily expenditures, recipes for ice cream and salad dressing. His garden book included the lives and deaths of flowers and vegetables.

Jefferson wrote more than eighteen thousand letters. There were love letters and letters to family members; letters to his children and grandchildren dispensing advice on schoolwork and behavior; letters to classmates and teachers; and letters to political colleagues. His correspondence was prolific and varied—a debate on the origins of the potato, a request for wine cuttings, practical advice, or a list of books for a private library. This list included such subjects as ancient and modern history, law, the physical sciences, politics, and religion, and classics such as the *Iliad* and the *Odyssey,* plays by Shakespeare and Molière, and novels by Jonathan Swift.

He created his own version of the Gospels and paraphrased the Psalms. He translated from French to English a commentary on Montesquieu's *The Spirit of Laws*. He drafted legal papers, including *A Summary View of the Rights of British America,* dubbed "Mr. Jefferson's Bill of Rights," which proposed intellectual justification for revolution and bearing arms; a constitution for Virginia; and the rules of procedure for Congress.

Jefferson was the author of one book: *Notes on the State of Virginia,* his answers to questions about his home state.

※ ※

A Recipe for Macaroni

- 6 eggs. yolks & whites.
- 2 wine glasses of milk
- 2 lb of flour
- a little salt

Work them together without water, and very well.

Roll it then with a roller to a paper thickness

Cut it into small pieces which roll again with the hand into long slips, & then cut them to a proper length.

Put them into warm water a quarter of an hour.

Drain them.

Dress them as maccaroni.

But if they are intended for soups they are to be put in the soup & not into warm water

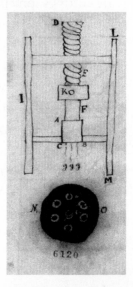

Jefferson's diagram of a "macaroni maker."

A Page from Jefferson's Garden Book

May. 27.
sowed Lettuce, Radish, Broccoli, & Cauliflower.

28.
Flower-de luces just opening.
*strawberries come to table. note this is the first year of their bearing having been planted in the spring of 1766. and on an average, the plants bear 20. strawberries each. 100 fill half a pint.
forwardest peas of March 17. come to table.
latest peas of Feb. 20. will come to table within about 4. days.
Snap-dragon blooming.

A Letter to a Granddaughter

My dear Cornelia

Monticello June 3. 11.

I have lately recieved a copy of mrs Edgeworth's Moral tales, which seeming better suited to your years than to mine, I inclose you the first volume. the other two shall follow as soon as your Mama has read them. they are to make a part of your library. . . . your family of silk worms is reduced to a single individual. . . . to encourage Virginia and Mary to take care of it, I tell them that as soon as they can get wedding gowns from this spinner they shall be married. I propose the same to you that, in order to hasten it's work, you may hasten home; for we all wish much to see you, and to express in person, rather than by letter, the assurance of our affectionate love.

Th. Jefferson

P.S. the girls desire me to add a postscript, to inform you that mrs Higginbotham has just given them new Dolls.

An Excerpt from *The Jefferson Bible: The Life and Morals of Jesus of Nazareth*

But I say unto you, That every idle word that men shall speak, they shall give account thereof in the day of judgment.

For by thy words thou shalt be justified, and by thy words thou shalt be condemned.

Therefore whosoever heareth these sayings of mine, and doeth them, I will liken him unto a wise man, which built his house upon a rock:

And the rain descended, and the floods came, and the winds blew, and beat upon that house; and it fell not: for it was founded upon a rock.

Jefferson's Poetry, a Paraphrased Version of Psalm 15

THE PORTRAIT OF A GOOD MAN BY THE MOST SUBLIME OF POETS, FOR YOUR IMITATION

Lord, who's the happy man that may to thy blest courts repair;

Not stranger-like to visit them, but to inhabit there?

'Tis he whose every thought and deed by rules of virtue moves;

Whose generous tongue disdains to speak the thing his heart disproves.

Who never did a slander forge, his neighbor's fame to wound;

Nor hearken to a false report, by malice whispered round.

Who vice in all its pomp and power, can treat with just neglect;

And piety, though clothed in rags, religiously respect.

Who to his plighted vows and trust has ever firmly stood;

And though he promise to his loss, he makes his promise good.

Whose soul in usury disdains his treasure to employ;

Whom no rewards can ever bribe the guiltless to destroy.

The man who by his steady course, has happiness insur'd.

When earth's foundations shake, shall stand, by Providence secur'd.

The Conclusion of Jefferson's
A Summary View of the Rights of British America, Addressed to George III

The whole art of government consists in the art of being honest. Only aim to do your duty, and mankind will give you credit where you fail. No longer persevere in sacrificing the rights of one part of the empire to the inordinate desires of another; but deal out to all equal and impartial right. . . . This is the important post in which fortune has placed you, holding the balance of a great, if a well poised empire.

※ ※

Some Rules of Procedure for Congress

- No Member shall read any printed paper in the House during the sitting thereof without Leave of the Congress.
- No Member in coming into the House or in removing from his Place shall pass between the President and the Member then speaking.
- When the House is sitting no Member shall speak [or whisper] to another as to interrupt any Member who may be speaking in the Debate.

※ ※

An Excerpt from Jefferson's
Notes on the State of Virginia

QUERY XVI
The measures taken with regard to the estates and possessions of the Rebels, commonly called Tories?

A tory has been properly defined to be a traitor in thought but not in deed. The only description, by which the laws have endeavored to come at them, was that of non-jurors, or persons refusing to take the oath of fidelity to the State. Persons of this description were at one time subjected to double taxation, at another to treble, and lastly were allowed retribution, and placed on a level with good citizens. It may be mentioned as a proof, both of the lenity of our government, and unanimity of its inhabitants, that though this war has now raged near seven years, not a single execution for treason has taken place.

An Excerpt from Jefferson's Autobiography, Detailing His Return from Paris

In the interval of my stay at home my eldest daughter had been happily married to the eldest son of the Tuckahoe branch of Randolphs, a young gentleman of genius, science and honorable mind, who afterwards filled a dignified station in the General Government, & the most dignified in his own State. I left Monticello on the 1st of March 1790. for New York. At Philadelphia I called on the venerable and beloved Franklin. He was then on the bed of sickness from which he never rose. My recent return from a country in which he had left so many friends, and the perilous convulsions to which they had been exposed, revived all his anxieties to know what part they had taken, what had been their course, and what their fate.

Jefferson's Advice from "A Decalogue of Canons for Observation in Practical Life"

1. Never put off till tomorrow what you can do today.
2. Never trouble another for what you can do yourself.
3. Never spend your money before you have it.
4. Never buy what you do not want, because it is cheap; it will be dear to you.
5. Pride costs us more than hunger, thirst, and cold.
6. We never repent of having eaten too little.
7. Nothing is troublesome that we do willingly.
8. How much pain have cost us the evils which have never happened.
9. Take things always by their smooth handle.
10. When angry, count ten before you speak; if very angry, a hundred.

"INVENTIONS"

The fact is, that one new idea leads to another, that to a third, and so on through a course of time until someone, with whom no one of these ideas is original, combines all together, and produces what is justly called a new invention.
—THOMAS JEFFERSON

Thomas Jefferson loved to design, improve, and figure out new ways to do things. He rarely came up with a true invention—that is, a brand-new idea that no one else had ever thought of. But he did create several improvements on common items and at least one genuine invention.

Automatic Doors

The glass doors in Monticello's parlor were linked by chains hidden under the floor, so that when one was opened or closed, the other followed, as if by magic.

Book Stand

Jefferson's book stand can hold five books at once, and turns so that all the books are easy to see and read.

Dumbwaiters

Set into each side of the fireplace in Monticello's dining room are dumbwaiters that bring up wine from the basement.

Five-sided book stand designed by Jefferson.

Great Clock

Jefferson designed the clock set above the entrance at Monticello, which is visible from both inside and outside. It is powered by a set of weights made of cannonballs from the Revolutionary War.

Lap Desk

A cabinetmaker in Philadelphia made this desk according to Jefferson's design, and Jefferson wrote the Declaration of Independence on it. It has storage space for pens and paper, and a hinged top that can be opened for writing or closed to use as a bookrest.

Jefferson's lap desk.

Moldboard

Jefferson was a farmer as well as a politician. His one actual invention was a new moldboard for a plow. A plow is used to dig and turn soil for planting; the moldboard is the curved part of the plow that turns the soil over. Jefferson's new moldboard was easy to use and "so light that two small horses or mules draw it with less labor."

Spherical Sundial

Jefferson's sundial had a sphere on the top, marked with the North and South Poles, the equator, and the meridian lines (which are drawn at equal intervals from one pole to the other). One meridian line (which was movable) cast a shadow that told the time. "My dial captivates every body foreign as well as home-bred, as a handsome object & accurate measurer of time," he said. Other spherical sundials had been made before, but Jefferson did not know about them. As far as historians can tell, he came up with the idea on his own.

Re-creation of Jefferson's spherical sundial.

Turning-Machine

Jefferson liked to show guests a revolving stand he had designed for his closet, to make it easy to choose his clothes.

Wheel Cipher

Jefferson's wheel cipher was designed to help spies or soldiers send secret messages. It was made up of twenty-six wooden disks that rotated around an iron pin. Each disk had the letters of the alphabet printed randomly around its edge. One person could write a message, and then use the spinning wheels to scramble it. The person who received the message would use another wheel cipher to unscramble the words. It is possible that Jefferson was the first person to think of a wheel cipher. Or he may have seen or heard of such devices and then created one of his own.

Re-creation of Jefferson's wheel cipher.

HOME

Virginia

Thomas Jefferson traveled to Europe and to many places within the United States, but Virginia was always home. His upbringing as the oldest son of a wealthy Virginian family influenced him greatly, and when his two terms as president of the United States were over, he returned to Virginia for good.

SHADWELL

Thomas Jefferson grew up at the Shadwell plantation. From his mother and his father, he learned how to manage the world around him, whether by surveying and mapping the wilderness or running a plantation worked by slaves.

WILLIAMSBURG

Williamsburg was the first place Jefferson encountered the wider world. He went to college there, studied and practiced law, and visited the royal governor in his mansion—a mansion where Jefferson himself would live when he became governor of Virginia in the midst of the American Revolution. In Williamsburg, Jefferson first encountered the ideas of the Enlightenment and took to heart the belief that humans should be ruled by reason and logic, not faith in the authority of kings, priests, or aristocrats.

At his plantation, Monticello, Jefferson planned everything. He selected the flowers in the garden, the wine that was served to his guests, the design of the parquet floor. Every detail was exactly what he wanted it to be.

Philadelphia, Pennsylvania

In a three-story house on the corner of Seventh and Market Streets, Thomas Jefferson settled into a private parlor across from his bedchamber to write the Declaration of Independence. Graff House, now known as the Declaration House, was rebuilt in 1975.

The declaration and the first constitution of the United States were read, debated, and signed in the Pennsylvania State House, now called Independence Hall. The famous Liberty Bell, hung in the State House, rang to announce to the citizens of Philadelphia that the Declaration of Independence had been signed.

Paris, France

Virginia was home, but France was marvelous. Thomas Jefferson adored the people, food, and culture of France. He loved shopping in Paris, where he bought paintings, statuary, furniture, books, and more. He saw plays, listened to concerts, and reveled in the gatherings of politicians, scientists, and influential men and women.

Washington, D.C.

Within Thomas Jefferson's lifetime the capital of the United States moved from Philadelphia, Pennsylvania, to Princeton, New Jersey; Annapolis, Maryland; Trenton, New Jersey; and New York, New York, before finally settling into a brand-new city on the Potomac River, created in 1790. The architect, Pierre Charles L'Enfant, designed the city with broad boulevards and wide public spaces like the ones in his hometown of Paris. But it took time for the city to fulfill L'Enfant's grand vision. By the end of Thomas Jefferson's two terms as president, only five thousand people lived in Washington. Some felt the city was too small, too primitive, and too unfinished. They wanted the nation's capital moved elsewhere—anywhere but the "wilderness city" or the "Capital of Miserable Huts." It never was. Washington, D.C., where Thomas Jefferson lived as vice president and president, is still the capital of the United States.

MONTICELLO

Jefferson was always happiest at his Virginia plantation, Monticello. He chose the site, designed the building (tearing down the first one and beginning again), furnished it with artwork and mementos of his long life, and entertained family and friends constantly. Monticello—Italian for "little mountain"—was Jefferson's own world.

The House

Work on Monticello began in 1768, when the site was leveled for building. Jefferson moved in two years later, but the house would not be entirely completed until 1809.

The mansion itself has forty-three rooms (not including the stables and space for carriages). Jefferson took painstaking care in decorating each room. The entrance hall displayed Native American artifacts, maps, paintings, and two engravings celebrating the Declaration of Independence. The parlor had a parquet floor that Jefferson designed himself, portraits of great figures in history, a piano, and a harpsichord. The bright yellow dining room had dumbwaiters that Jefferson designed to bring wine up from the cellar. There was also a revolving serving door with shelves on one side. Dishes were brought up from the kitchen and placed on the shelves. Once the door was spun around, the dishes could be quickly placed on the table.

There were three indoor toilets in Monticello, at a time when this was uncommon in America. Thomas Jefferson would likely have encountered flushing indoor toilets during his time in Europe. The toilets at Monticello, however, did not flush. Waste was probably collected in chamber pots and removed.

The Grounds and Gardens

Jefferson adored his gardens and took careful note of how the flowers, fruits, and vegetables were faring. The oval-shaped West Lawn was a favorite playground for his grandchildren. A winding walk was bordered with flowers of Jefferson's choice, and cared for by his daughters and granddaughters; other oval flower beds were planted with tulips, hyacinths, and anemones, among many others. Jefferson's fruit garden provided delicacies for the table and allowed him to experiment with over 150 varieties of fruit. There were apricots, almonds, figs, cherries, strawberries, currants, gooseberries, and raspberries, along with apples and peaches for making cider and brandy. The vegetable gardens took up about two acres, and Jefferson tried growing squash and broccoli imported from Italy, figs from France, peppers from Mexico, twenty kinds of beans, and fifteen types of peas.

Mulberry Row

Monticello required a lot of labor, and many of the people who made the plantation function lived on Mulberry Row. Free whites and blacks who were employed at Monticello, indentured servants, and slaves all lived here. As well as providing housing for the workers, Mulberry Row included a joiner's workshop, where carpenters made furniture, carriages, and necessary items for the mansion, such as doors and window sashes. There was also a workshop for making the cotton and wool that clothed the plantation's slaves, a nailery where enslaved boys produced nails, a blacksmith's shop, a smokehouse, a dairy, a stable, and a washhouse for laundry.

FINDING JEFFERSON TODAY IN THE UNITED STATES AND FRANCE

United States

MISSOURI

Gateway Arch and Jefferson National Expansion Memorial, St. Louis
St. Louis is very near the starting point of Lewis and Clark's Corps of Discovery expedition. The Gateway Arch is the centerpiece of the Jefferson National Expansion Memorial.

NEW YORK

57 Maiden Lane, New York
The home (no longer in existence) where Thomas Jefferson resided for the majority of his time in New York City. It was located in the present-day Financial District. The site eventually became the headquarters of Home Insurance Company, which installed a plaque in 1929, commemorating Thomas Jefferson's time there.

United States Military Academy at West Point
In 1802, Jefferson founded the United States Military Academy, the premier four-year service academy of the U.S. Army. He wanted to cement the importance of "useful

sciences" in American education, and hoped to create young representatives of democratic society. Today the entire central campus is a national landmark.

OREGON AND WASHINGTON

Lewis and Clark National Historical Park

Meriwether Lewis and William Clark were commissioned by Thomas Jefferson in 1803 to explore the uncharted West with the hope of finding a transcontinental route and natural resources. This park commemorates their journey. It is also the site of Fort Clatsop National Memorial, a replica of the winter encampment of Lewis and Clark's Corps of Discovery. It sits at the mouth of the Columbia River in Oregon. The pine tree overlooking the Pacific Ocean where William Clark carved his name has been cut down.

PENNSYLVANIA

American Philosophical Society, Philadelphia

Jefferson was elected to the American Philosophical Society in 1780. In 1781, he was made a Counsellor. Jefferson had many goals for his time in the society, including the study of the Hessian fly and finding an entire skeleton of a mammoth. The society also supported Jefferson's dispatching the Lewis and Clark expedition. Jefferson served as president of the American Philosophical Society for eighteen years.

Congress Hall, Philadelphia
Built in the late 1780s, this building was the meeting place of the U.S. Congress from 1790 to 1800. As vice president from 1797 to 1801, Jefferson presided over the Senate here.

SOUTH DAKOTA

Mount Rushmore, Keystone
Mount Rushmore is composed of the likenesses of four great presidents: George Washington, Thomas Jefferson, Abraham Lincoln, and Theodore Roosevelt. In the heart of the Black Hills, artist Gutzon Borglum and more than 350 workers sculpted these faces into the mountain. Borglum accomplished 90 percent of the monument with dynamite.

VIRGINIA

Poplar Forest, Bedford County
Poplar Forest was Jefferson's personal retreat. Construction of the house and grounds began in 1806. After he retired at age sixty-five, Jefferson spent much of his time there, appreciating the privacy and the quiet time with his family and his thoughts.

University of Virginia, Charlottesville

In 1818, Jefferson began an undertaking that would make use of his political, intellectual, and architectural skills— the founding of a university. In Jefferson's own words, the mission of the University of Virginia was to "form the statesmen, legislators and judges, on whom public prosperity, and individual happiness are so much to depend."

WASHINGTON, D.C.

Jefferson Memorial

Located on the southern end of the National Mall, the Jefferson Memorial contains a nineteen-foot statue of Jefferson, as well as phrases carved into the panels on the walls. President Franklin D. Roosevelt laid the cornerstone in 1939, but the memorial was not dedicated until 1943. More than two million people visit the Jefferson Memorial every year.

Library of Congress

During the War of 1812, British troops burned roughly three thousand books belonging to Congress. Jefferson offered to sell the nation his own collection, made up of 6,487 volumes. These texts formed the core of the new Library of Congress. Today the Thomas Jefferson Building is the central building of the Library of Congress.

France

Champs-Elyseés and Rue de Berri, Paris

On this corner in Paris, a plaque marks where Thomas Jefferson resided for most of the five years he served as U.S. minister to France. His house was called the Hôtel de Langeac and has since been demolished. The plaque was a gift from alumni of the University of Virginia.

Thomas Jefferson Statue, Paris

Located at the Quai Anatole France on Paris's Left Bank, this statue commemorates Thomas Jefferson's time as a statesman in France. It is near the Hotel de Salm, now the Palais de la Legion d'Honneur, which was an inspiration for the second version of Monticello.

RECOMMENDED READING

Aronson, Marc. *The Real Revolution: The Global Story of American Independence*. New York: Clarion Books, 2005.

Blair, Margaret Whitman. *Liberty or Death: The Surprising Story of Runaway Slaves Who Sided with the British During the American Revolution*. Washington, DC: National Geographic Children's Books, 2010.

Blumberg, Rhoda. *The Incredible Journey of Lewis and Clark*. New York: HarperCollins Publishers, 1995.

———. *York's Adventures with Lewis and Clark: An African-American's Part in the Great Expedition*. New York: HarperCollins Publishers, 2006.

Bradley, Kimberly Brubaker. *Jefferson's Sons: A Founding Father's Secret Children*. New York: Puffin Books, 2013.

Chew, Elizabeth V. *Thomas Jefferson: A Day at Monticello*. Illus. Mark Elliott. New York: Abrams, 2014.

Fradin, Dennis Brindell. *The Signers: The 56 Stories Behind the Declaration of Independence*. Illus. Michael McCurdy. New York: Bloomsbury, 2003.

Freedman, Russell. *Give Me Liberty! The Story of the Declaration of Independence*. New York: Holiday House, 2000.

———. *Lafayette and the American Revolution*. New York: Holiday House, 2010.

Harness, Cheryl. *Thomas Jefferson*. Washington, DC: National Geographic Children's Books, 2004.

Kalman, Maira. *Thomas Jefferson: Life, Liberty and the Pursuit of Everything*. New York: Penguin, 2014.

Lanier, Shannon, and Jane Feldman. *Jefferson's Children: The Story of One American Family*. New York: Random House Books for Young Readers, 2000.

Meltzer, Milton. *The American Revolutionaries: A History in Their Own Words, 1750–1800*. New York: HarperCollins, 1993.

Murphy, Jim. *A Young Patriot: The American Revolution as Experienced by One Boy*. New York: Clarion Books, 1996.

Norwich, Grace. *I Am Sacagawea*. Illus. Anthony VanArsdale. New York: Scholastic, 2012.

Rosenstock, Barb. *Thomas Jefferson Builds a Library*. Illus. John O'Brien. Honesdale, Pennsylvania: Highlights, 2013.

Schanzer, Rosalyn. *George vs. George: The American Revolution as Seen from Both Sides*. Washington, DC: National Geographic Children's Books, 2004.

———. *How We Crossed the West: The Adventures of Lewis & Clark*. Washington, DC: National Geographic Children's Books, 1997.

RECOMMENDED WEBSITES

Declaration of Independence

classroom.monticello.org/kids/resources/profile/6/Jefferson-and-the
-Declaration-of-Independence/

Lewis and Clark

LEWIS AND CLARK ACTIVITIES
teacher.scholastic.com/activities/lewis_clark/prepare.htm

LEWIS AND CLARK MAPPING THE WEST
mnh.si.edu/education/lc/lcmapping

LEWIS AND CLARK AS NATURALISTS
mnh.si.edu/lewisandclark/index.html

LEWIS AND CLARK'S HISTORIC TRAIL
lewisclark.net

NATIONAL GEOGRAPHIC INTERACTIVE JOURNEY LOG
nationalgeographic.com/lewisandclark

Library of Congress

JEFFERSON'S LIBRARY
loc.gov/exhibits/jefferson/jefflib.html

Smithsonian

MR. PRESIDENT
smithsonianeducation.org/president/gallerymain.aspx

THOMAS JEFFERSON
americanhistory.si.edu/presidency/5c_frame.html

Thomas Jefferson Foundation/Monticello

CLASSROOM SITE FOR KIDS
classroom.monticello.org/kids/home

MONTICELLO
monticello.org

University of Virginia

THOMAS JEFFERSON DIGITAL ARCHIVE
guides.lib.virginia.edu/TJ

NOTES

Abbreviations Used

APE: Gil Troy, Arthur M. Schlesinger Jr., and Fred L. Israel, eds., *History of American Presidential Elections, 1789–2008*, 4th ed., Vol. 1, *1789–1868*.

EOL: Gordon S. Wood, *Empire of Liberty: A History of the Early Republic, 1789–1815*.

FB: Thomas Jefferson's Farm Book: With Commentary and Relevant Extracts from Other Writings, ed. Edwin Morris Betts.

GB: Thomas Jefferson's Garden Book: 1766–1824, With Relevant Extracts from His Other Writings, ed. Edwin Morris Betts.

Jefferson: Thomas Jefferson, *Writings*, ed. Merrill D. Peterson (Library of America).

JHT: Dumas Malone, *Jefferson and His Time*, I–VI.

LOC: Library of Congress.

MB: Jefferson's Memorandum Books: Accounts, with Legal Records and Miscellany, 1767–1826, ed. James A. Bear Jr. and Lucia C. Stanton.

PTJ: The Papers of Thomas Jefferson, I–XXXIX.

PTJRS: The Papers of Thomas Jefferson, Retirement Series, I–VIII.

Randall: Henry S. Randall, *The Life of Thomas Jefferson*, I–III.

TDLTJ: Sarah N. Randolph, *The Domestic Life of Thomas Jefferson*.

TJF: The Thomas Jefferson Foundation.

VTM: Merrill D. Peterson, *Visitors to Monticello*.

PROLOGUE

"the world's best hope" *PTJ*, XXXIII, 149.

"Whatever they can, they will" *PTJRS*, VIII, 32.

"Oh, I thought you knew the Squire" *TDLTJ*, 38.

CHAPTER ONE

"It is the strong in body" *TDLTJ*, 20.

fought off "the attacks" Ibid.

Finding a wild turkey "Memoir of Thomas Jefferson Randolph," Edgehill-Randolph Papers, Collection 1397, Box 11, University of Virginia.

"the youth of these more indulgent settlements" Edmund S. Morgan, *Virginians at Home: Family Life in the Eighteenth Century* (Charlottesville, VA, 1963), 7.

"constant companion when home" Randall, I, 40–41.

"Many a winter evening" *TDLTJ*, 34.

"from the time when" Ibid., 37.

"It is a charming thing" *PTJ*, XXXVII, 20.

"The parent storms" Jefferson, 288.

"At 14 years of age" *TDLTJ*, 26.

"She was an agreeable" Randall, I, 16–17.

"to which the privilege" Kevin J. Hayes, *The Road to Monticello: The Life and Mind of Thomas Jefferson* (Oxford, 2008), 36.

"By going to the College" *PTJ*, I, 3.

"have made due progress" Hayes, *The Road to Monticello*, 47.

CHAPTER TWO

"The best news I can tell you" John J. Reardon, *Peyton Randolph, 1721–1775: One Who Presided* (Durham, NC, 1982), 39.

"Knowledge" *PTJ*, X, 308.

"It was my great good fortune" Jefferson, 4.

"to me . . . a father" *PTJRS*, VIII, 200.

"of the middle size" *TDLTJ*, 30.

"Mr. Wythe continued" Ibid., 28.

"an elegant set of" Imogene E. Brown, *American Aristides: A Biography of George Wythe* (Rutherford, NJ, 1981), 81–82.

"Mrs. Wythe puts" Ibid., 82.

"the construction of a wheel" *TDLTJ*, 37–38.

"walking encyclopedia" Ibid., 37.

"no useful object" *MB*, I, 338.

"Not less than two hours" *PTJ*, X, 308.

"I was often thrown" Randall, I, 22–23.

"large in size" Ibid., 51.

"Under temptations and difficulties" Ibid., 22.

"I am convinced" *TDLTJ*, 284.

"informs the mind" John P. Kaminski, ed., *The Founders on the Founders: Word Portraits from the American Revolutionary Era* (Charlottesville, VA, 2008), 291.

"Is there any such thing" *PTJ*, I, 3–5.

"All things here" Ibid., 7.

"I was prepared" *PTJ*, I, 11.

"a few broken sentences" Ibid.

"opened my mind" Ibid., 13–14.

"I asked no question" Ibid., 14.

CHAPTER THREE
"Our minds were circumscribed" Jefferson, 5.

"He was ready to ask pardon" *Journal of a French Traveller in the Colonies, 1765*, I, 745.

"I went there in expectation" Ibid., 746.

"to subjects most familiar" Randall, I, 45.

"a most intelligent" Ibid., 45–46.

"Ah, Joanna" *MB*, I, 247. See also Hayes, *Road to Monticello*, 87–88.

"Purple hyacinth" *GB*, 1.

"greatly endanger[ing]" *PTJ*, I, 19.

"no face known" Ibid.

"extremely beautiful" Ibid.

"very little the air" Ibid., 19–20.

"in all cases whatsoever" Edmund S. Morgan and Helen M. Morgan, *The Stamp Act Crisis: Prologue to Revolution* (Chapel Hill, NC, 1995), 288.

CHAPTER FOUR
"You will perceive that" *JHT*, I, 448.

"We had previously" Ibid., 449.

"with indignation" Ibid.

"I have heard" Ibid., 136.

"Run away" *PTJ*, I, 33.

"I made one effort" Jefferson, 5.

"Everyone comes into" Annette Gordon-Reed, *The Hemingses of Monticello: An American Family* (New York, 2008), 100.

"But, ah!" *TDLTJ*, 43.

CHAPTER FIVE
"Harmony in the marriage" *PTJ*, XXX, 15.

"Her complexion was brilliant" Randall, I, 63–64.

"good sense and good nature" *PTJ*, I, 66.

"Let the case be" Ibid., 71.

"border on tartness" *TJF*, www .monticello.org/site/jefferson/martha -wayles-skelton-jefferson.

"Much better" *PTJ*, XXX, 15.

"An elegant building" Susan R. Stein, *The Worlds of Thomas Jefferson at Monticello* (New York, 1993), 14.

"The horrible dreariness" Randall, I, 64.

"lit up with song" Ibid., 65.

"Mrs. Jefferson would" James A. Bear Jr., ed., *Jefferson at Monticello* (Charlottesville, VA, 1967), 3.

"As all Virginians" *VTM*, 9.

CHAPTER SIX
"Blows must decide" John Ferling, *Almost a Miracle: The American Victory in the War of Independence* (New York, 2009), 28.

"a day of general" *PTJ*, I, 106.

"The effects of the day[s]" Jefferson, 9.

"that our ancestors" Ibid., 105–6.

"It is neither our wish" Ibid., 121–22.

"by any power on earth" Ibid.

"Let those flatter" Ibid., 121.

"Mr. Jefferson's Bill" *PTJ*, I, 672.

"a very handsome public paper" Randall, I, 188.

"Tamer sentiments" Ibid., 90.

"Gentlemen may cry" Henry Mayer, *A Son of Thunder: Patrick Henry and the American Republic* (New York, 2001), 245.

"impressive and sublime" *The Writings and Speeches of Daniel Webster*, XVII, ed. Fletcher Webster (Boston, 1903), 367.

"that every horseman" *PTJ*, I, 161.

"Force should be repelled" Robert Middlekauff, *The Glorious Cause: The American Revolution, 1763–1789* (New York, 2005), 272.

"last hopes of reconciliation" Ibid., 281.

"A frenzy of revenge" Ibid., 279.

"one of the highest insults" Michael A. McDonnell, *The Politics of War: Race, Class, and Conflict in Revolutionary Virginia* (Chapel Hill, NC, 2007), 52–54.

"declare freedom to the slaves" Ibid., 55.

"A little knowledge" *PTJ*, I, 165–66.

CHAPTER SEVEN

"As our enemies have found" *PTJ*, I, 186.

"the famous Mr. Jefferson" Hayes, *Road to Monticello*, 167.

"Nobody now entertains" *PTJ*, I, 186.

"a small faction" Ibid., 241.

"They have taken it" Ibid.

"My collection" Ibid., 242–43.

"Though we may politically differ" Ibid., 244.

"I have never received" Ibid., 252.

"The plan is to lay waste" Ibid., 247.

"We care not for our towns" Ibid., 259.

CHAPTER EIGHT

"The bells rung" Harlow Giles Unger, *John Hancock: Merchant King and American Patriot* (New York, 2000), 242.

"obliged to avoid reading" *PTJ*, VI, 570.

"I am here" Ibid., I, 292.

"United Colonies" Ibid., 298–99.

"It was thought" Ibid., 313.

"I consider you and him" David McCullough, *John Adams* (New York, 2001), 604.

"Mr. Jefferson came into" *The Works of John Adams*, II, ed. Charles Francis Adams (Boston, 1856), 513.

"I will not" Ibid.

"not to find out" TJ to Henry Lee, May 8, 1825. Extract published at Papers of Thomas Jefferson: Retirement Series Digital Archive, www.monticello.org/familyletters (accessed 2011).

"intended to be" Ibid.

"When in the course of human events" *PTJ*, I, 315, 413–33.

"God bless the free states" William Hogeland, *Declaration: The Nine Tumultuous Weeks When America Became Independent, May 1–July 4, 1776* (New York, 2010), 179.

CHAPTER NINE

"I pray you to come" *PTJ*, I, 477.

"I wish I could" Ibid., 458.

"No Member shall" Ibid., 456–58.

"Our camps recruit slowly" Ibid., 477.

"the Jew and the Gentile" Jefferson, 34.

"born after a certain day" Ibid., 44.

"deportation at a proper age" Ibid.

"It was found that" Ibid.

"Nothing is more certainly" Ibid.

"Two races, equally free" Ibid.

"While we are" *PTJ*, III, 447.

"In ten minutes" Bear, *Jefferson at Monticello*, 7–8.

"He's gone to the mountains" Ibid., 8.

"like an earthquake" Ibid., 9.

CHAPTER TEN

"Such terror and confusion" *JHT*, I, 358–59.

"There being nothing" Virginia Scharff, *The Women Jefferson Loved* (New York, 2010), 139.

"cruelly lashed" Virginius Dabney, "Jouett Outrides Tarleton, and Saves Jefferson from Capture," *Scribner's Magazine*, June 1928, 691–2.

"Fire away, then" Michael Kranish, *Flight from Monticello: Thomas Jefferson at War* (New York, 2010), 284.

"treasons of the heart" *PTJ*, VI, 185.

"She has been" Ibid., 186.

"was never out of calling" *TDLTJ*, 63.

"Her eyes ever rested" Randall, I, 380.

"When she came to the children" Bear, *Jefferson at Monticello*, 99–100.

"The violence of his emotion" *TDLTJ*, 63.

"I was never a moment" Ibid.

"In those melancholy rambles" Ibid.

"To the memory of" Randall, I, 383.

CHAPTER ELEVEN

"The states will go to war" *PTJ*, VI, 248.

"We have some hopes" Ibid., 381.

"all the good citizens" Ibid., 463.

"I find they have subscribed" Ibid., 371.

"the different species" Ibid.

"will render you more" Ibid., 359.

"the following is" Ibid., 360.

"I suppose the crippled state" Ibid., VII, 25.

"though they have made peace" Ibid., 15–16.

"good company" *TDLTJ*, 73.

"the most agreeable country" Roy Moore and Alma Moore, *Thomas Jefferson's Journey to the South of France* (New York, 1999), 16.

"a house of education" *PTJ*, XI, 612.

"For the articles of household furniture" Ibid., VIII, 230.

"Mr. Adams's colleague" L. H. Butterfield, Wendell D. Garrett, and Marjorie E. Sprague, eds., *Adams Family Correspondence*, VI, 78.

"every day enlarging" William Howard Adams, *The Paris Years of Thomas Jefferson* (New Haven, CT, 2000), 41.

this "great and good" country Jefferson, 98.

"So ask the travelled inhabitant" Ibid.

"to purchase their peace" *PTJ*, VII, 511.

"It is said that Great Britain" Ibid., VIII, 196.

"A most unfortunate" Ibid., VII, 441.

"both suffered as much pain" Ibid., 441–42.

"kiss my dear, dear Polly" Ibid., 636.

"I must have Polly" Ibid., VIII, 141.

CHAPTER TWELVE
"We have no rose" *PTJ*, X, 451.

"I need not tell you" Ibid., IX, 318.

"I have heard them say" *MB*, I, 610.

"I am savage" *PTJ*, VIII, 500.

"He is everything" Kaminski, *Founders on the Founders*, 293.

"Dear Papa" *PTJ*, VIII, 517.

"I wish so much to see you" Ibid., 532–33.

"golden-haired, languishing" Helen Duprey Bullock, *My Head and My Heart: A Little History of Thomas Jefferson and Maria Cosway* (New York, 1945), 14.

"It will be with infinite pleasure" *PTJ*, X, 433.

"Well, friend" Ibid., 444.

"I tell her that I did not" Gordon-Reed, *Hemingses of Monticello*, 502.

"Thrown into all" Ibid., 551.

CHAPTER THIRTEEN
"He desired to bring my mother" Jan Ellen Lewis and Peter S. Onuf, eds., *Sally Hemings and Thomas Jefferson: History, Memory, and Civic Culture* (Charlottesville, VA, 1999), 256.

"Don't be alarmed" *PTJ*, X, 557.

"I can never fear" Ibid., 619.

"It really is" Ibid., XII, 69.

"How do you like" Ibid., 350–51.

"freedom of religion" Ibid., 440.

"We have had 13 states" Ibid., 356–57.

"It is my principle" Ibid., 442.

"There are indeed some faults" Ibid., XIII, 174.

"The ground of liberty" Ibid., XVI, 129.

"His Highness" Ibid., XV, 147–48.

"Always an honest man" Ibid., 315.

"at this moment there is not" Douglas Brymner, *Report on Canadian Archives, 1890* (Ottawa, 1891), 97–98. Lord Dorchester sent this report to Lord Sydney on April 10, 1787.

"Paris is now become" *PTJ*, XIII, 151.

"A more dangerous scene of war" Ibid., XV, 279.

"break every engagement" Ibid., 354.

"a silent witness" Ibid., 355.

"So far it seemed" Ibid., XVI, 293.

"She was just beginning" Lewis and Onuf, *Sally Hemings and Thomas Jefferson*, 256.

"extraordinary privileges" Ibid.

"Jefferson was the father" Ibid.

CHAPTER FOURTEEN

"In general" *PTJ*, XVI, 493.

"fine autumn weather" Ibid., XV, 552.

"My great wish" Ibid., XIV, 651.

"Mr. Jefferson is here" Lester J. Cappon, ed., *The Adams-Jefferson Letters: The Complete Correspondence Between Thomas Jefferson and Abigail and John Adams* (Chapel Hill, NC, 1987), xxxix.

"Nothing can excel" *PTJ*, XIV, 223.

"He was incapable of fear" *PTJRS*, VII, 101.

"through with his purpose" Ibid.

"His mind was great" Ibid.

"His temper was naturally" Ibid.

"Be so good as" *PTJ*, XVI, 286.

"If the Duke" Ibid., XII, 220–21.

"if we could be smitten" Ibid., XIII, 461–62.

"I have always preferred" Julian P. Boyd, *Number 7: Alexander Hamilton's Secret Attempts to Control American Foreign Policy, with Supporting Documents* (Princeton, NJ, 1964), 24.

"it would be the most perfect" *PTJRS*, III, 305.

"Opposed in death" Randall, III, 336.

"We were all strongly attached to France" *EOL*, 174–75.

"In the struggle which was necessary" *PTJ*, XXV, 14.

CHAPTER FIFTEEN

"I live on my horse" *PTJ*, XXVIII, 332.

"For I will frankly" Ibid., XXIV, 499.

"to prepare the way" Ibid., XXIII, 537.

"he did not like" Ibid., 263.

"The confidence of the whole union" Ibid., 539.

"had pressed . . . a continuance" Ibid., XXV, 244.

"a thousand others" Ibid.

"From Monticello you" Ibid., 444.

"Worn out" Ibid., XXVI, 240–41.

"with sincere regret" Ibid., XXVIII, 3.

"Jefferson went off" *The Words of Thomas Jefferson* (Charlottesville, VA, 2008), 201.

"Architecture is my delight" *JHT,* III, 222.

"Every article is" *FB,* xiv.

"below the old dam" *TJF,* www .monticello.org/site/research-and -collections/fishing (accessed 2012).

"He has not worn his shoes" *PTJ,* XXVIII, 249.

"My private business" Ibid., 14.

"A change so extraordinary" Ibid., 41.

"The attempt which has been made" Ibid., 219.

"the people of this State" *APE,* 169.

"I have not the arrogance" Ibid., 199.

CHAPTER SIXTEEN

"There is a debt of service" *PTJ,* XXIX, 233.

"for no one can know" Ibid., 193.

"monarchist" John Ferling, *Adams vs. Jefferson: The Tumultuous Election of 1800* (New York, 2004), 90.

"I do sincerely wish" *PTJ,* XXIX, 211.

"He has always been my senior" Ibid., 223.

"He said that if Mr. Madison" Ibid., 552.

"The second office" Ibid., 362.

"going on with excuses" Ibid., 552.

"the half-war with France" *EOL,* 245.

"write, print, utter or publish" Ibid., 259.

"As president" James Morton Smith, *Freedom's Fetters: The Alien and Sedition Laws and American Civil Liberties* (Ithaca, NY, 1966), 339.

"cannot fail to produce" *APE,* 63.

"If this goes down" *PTJ,* XXX, 560.

"I have been for some time" Ibid., 129.

"No one can know" Gaillard Hunt, ed., *The First Forty Years of Washington Society in the Family Letters of Margaret Bayard Smith* (New York, 1965), 406.

"A determination never to do" Randall, I, 22–23.

CHAPTER SEVENTEEN

"It is extremely uncertain" Herbert A. Johnson, ed., and others, *The Papers of John Marshall,* VI (Chapel Hill, NC, 1974), 41.

"Perhaps no man in this community" *JHT,* III, 443.

"In times like this" *APE,* 61.

"which I think" Ibid.

"Well, I understand" *PTJRS,* III, 306.

"I believe we may consider" *PTJ,* XXXII, 300.

"The election" Ibid., 385.

"There would be really cause" Susan Dunn, *Jefferson's Second Revolution: The Election Crisis of 1800 and the Triumph of Republicanism* (Boston, 2004), 198.

"What will be the plans" Ibid., 204.

"He grew warm" *PTJRS*, III, 306.

"I long to be" *PTJ*, XXXII, 475.

"Jefferson is to be preferred" *JHT*, III, 500.

"made me a visit" McCullough, *John Adams*, 559.

"unite in himself" *EOL*, 283.

"I sincerely thank you" *PTJ*, XXXIII, 422.

CHAPTER EIGHTEEN

"It must be admitted" *PTJ*, XXXIII, 127.

"All . . . will bear in mind" Ibid., 149–51.

"a pledge to the community" Dunn, *Jefferson's Second Revolution*, 225.

"old friends who had been" *PTJ*, XXXIII, 261.

"I sincerely wish" Ibid., 426.

"I feel a great load" Ibid., 181.

"This whole chapter" Ibid., 394.

"No more good" Ibid., 506.

"*Politics* will not make you" Ibid., 568.

"May none but Honest" Frank Freidel and Hugh Sidey, *The Presidents of the United States of America* (White House Historical Association, 2006), whitehouse.gov/about/presidents/johnadams

"water closets . . . of superior construction" William Seale, *The President's House: A History*, I (Washington, DC, 1986), 88.

"I now begin" *PTJ*, XXXIII, 575.

"he was in possession" Fawn M. Brodie, *Thomas Jefferson: An Intimate History* (New York, 1998), 345–46.

"By this means" *PTJ*, XXXV, 576–78.

"a steady and uniform course" Ibid., 677.

"4 hours for riding" Ibid.

"engaged with company" Ibid., XXXVI, 99.

"mechanics, mathematics, philosophy" TJ to Thomas Paine, January 13, 1803, Thomas Jefferson Papers, LOC.

"the president's dinners" Noble E. Cunningham, *The Jeffersonian Republicans in Power: Party Operations, 1801–1809* (Chapel Hill, NC, 1963), 96.

"Mr. Jefferson has put aside" Louis-André Pichon to Ministère des Affaires étrangères, 26 Pluviôse an 10, *Correspondance Politique*, vol. 54, Les Archives Diplomatiques.

"The door opened suddenly" Augustus Foster to Elizabeth Cavendish, December 30, 1804, Augustus Foster Papers, LOC.

"You know Virginians" *JHT*, IV, 373.

"Why are these libels allowed?" Margaret Bayard Smith, *First Forty Years*, 397.

"Put that paper in your pocket" Ibid.

"by sinking, burning, or destroying" Abraham D. Sofaer, *War, Foreign Affairs, and Constitutional Power: The Origins* (Cambridge, MA, 1976), 209.

"alarm all who are anxious" Claude G. Bowers, *Jefferson in Power: The Death Struggle of the Federalists* (Boston, 1936), 90.

"Mine is an odd destiny" Ibid., 94–95.

"Burr will doubtless" *Life and Correspondence of Rufus King*, IV, ed. Charles R. King (New York, 1971), 103–4.

"Capt. Lewis is brave" *PTJ*, XXXIX, 599.

CHAPTER NINETEEN

"Every face" Andrew Jackson to TJ, August 7, 1803, Thomas Jefferson Papers, LOC.

"that your Excellency" *PTJ*, XXXV, 477.

"to go to Washington" Ibid., XXXVI, 581.

"It is well known that" Ibid., XXXVIII, 323–25.

"Callender and Sally" McCullough, *John Adams*, 581.

"beautiful, simplicity and timidity" Smith, *First Forty Years*, 34.

"so eagerly and noisily" Ibid., 396.

"Adieu once more" *PTJ*, XXXIX, 309–10.

"I am willing to hope" Joseph J. Ellis, *American Creation: Triumphs and Tragedies at the Founding of the Republic* (New York, 2007), 212–13.

"There is on the globe one single spot" *PTJ*, XXXVII, 264.

"Spain might have retained it" Ibid.

"The day that France takes possession" Ibid.

"You will have no need" Ellis, *American Creation*, 220–21.

"I renounce Louisiana" Ibid.

"It is something larger" TJ to Thomas Mann Randolph Jr., July 5, 1803, Thomas Jefferson Papers, LOC.

"This removes from us" Ibid.

"It must . . . strike" Horatio Gates to TJ, July 7, 1803, Thomas Jefferson Papers, LOC.

"Every face" Andrew Jackson to TJ, August 7, 1803, Thomas Jefferson Papers, LOC.

"great and weighty matters" Proclamation for Special Session of Congress, 1803, portfolio 227, no. 3, Broadside Collection, LOC.

CHAPTER TWENTY

"If we can keep" TJ to Elbridge Gerry, March 3, 1804, Thomas Jefferson Papers, LOC.

"The principle of society" TJ to William Short, January 23, 1804, John Work Garrett Library, Johns Hopkins University, Baltimore.

"was excellent" TJF, www .monticello.org/site/research-and -collections/dinner-etiquette (accessed 2011).

"And must we" Timothy Pickering to Theodore Lyman, February 11, 1804, Timothy Pickering Papers, Massachusetts Historical Society.

"It is not unusual" Ibid.

"I feel dreadfully" John Wayles Eppes to TJ, March 19, 1804, Edgehill-Randolph Papers, University of Virginia.

"How the President" Thomas Mann Randolph Jr. to Caesar A. Rodney, April 16, 1804, Andre De Coppet Collection, Princeton University.

"But I know how closely" Abigail Adams to TJ, May 20, 1804, Literary & Historical Manuscripts, The Morgan Library & Museum, New York.

"Each of us, perhaps" *JHT*, IV, 430.

"Clinton's family and connections" Bowers, *Jefferson in Power*, 257–58.

"All is now business" TJ to John Glendy, March 3, 1805, Thomas Jefferson Papers, LOC.

"Genl. Washington" TJ to John Taylor, January 6, 1805, Thomas Jefferson Papers, LOC.

"hopes of complete success" William Clark to TJ, April 3, 1805, Thomas Jefferson Papers, LOC.

"The voyage of discovery" William Eustis to TJ, August 17, 1805, Thomas Jefferson Papers, LOC.

"Capt William Clark" John Bakeless, ed., *The Journals of Lewis and Clark* (New York, 2002), 283.

"one horn of a colossal animal" TJ to Caspar Wistar Jr., March 20, 1808, Thomas Jefferson Papers, LOC.

"I would recommend" Zebulon Pike to TJ, February 3, 1808, Papers of Thomas Jefferson: Editorial Files, Princeton University.

"I put them together while here" TJ to Charles Willson Peale, February 6, 1808, Thomas Jefferson Papers, LOC.

"is well-placed to be considered" Edward Thornton to Lord Hawkesbury, August 4, 1802, FO 5/35, National Archives of the United Kingdom, Kew.

"Our constitution is" *JHT*, V, 76.

"What an awful spectacle" TJ to Thomas Lomax, January 11, 1806, Thomas Jefferson Papers, LOC.

"quiet, at home at least" Ibid.

CHAPTER TWENTY-ONE

"Never since" TJ to Pierre-Samuel du Pont de Nemours, July 14, 1807, Thomas Jefferson Papers, LOC.

"a fashionable wig" Martha Jefferson Randolph to TJ, October 26, 1805, Coolidge Collection of Thomas Jefferson Manuscripts, Massachusetts Historical Society.

"This is indeed" James Wilkinson to TJ, November 12, 1806, in *Report of the Committee Appointed to Inquire into the Conduct of General Wilkinson* (Washington, DC, 1811), 425–28.

"in cases of insurrection" TJ to John Dawson, December 19, 1806, Thomas Jefferson Papers, LOC.

"I do not believe" TJ to George Hay, June 20, 1807, Thomas Jefferson Papers, LOC.

"The nation will judge" TJ to William Branch Giles, April 20, 1807, Thomas Jefferson Papers, LOC.

"I am now in the 7th day" TJ to Martha Jefferson Randolph, March 20, 1807, Edgehill-Randolph Papers, University of Virginia Library.

"I am tired of" TJ to John Dickinson, January 13, 1807, Historical Society of Pennsylvania.

"making every preparation" Message to Congress, December 17, 1807, LOC.

"Governmental prohibitions" Albert Gallatin to TJ, December 18, 1807, Thomas Jefferson Papers, LOC.

"This gives time" TJ to John Taylor, January 6, 1808, Washburn Collection, Massachusetts Historical Society.

"I have been happy" TJ to Thomas Leiper, May 25, 1808, Thomas Jefferson Papers, LOC.

"You infernal villain" John Lane Jones to TJ, August 8, 1808, Thomas Jefferson Collection, HM 9018, The Huntington Library, San Marino, CA.

"the attempt is" James Sullivan to TJ, April 2, 1808, Thomas Jefferson Papers, LOC.

CHAPTER TWENTY-TWO

"Amidst the din of war" *PTJRS*, I, 359.

"I am already sensible" TJ to Charles Thomson, December 25, 1808, Charles Thomson Papers, LOC.

"Nature intended me" TJ to Pierre-Samuel du Pont de Nemours, March 2, 1809, Thomas Jefferson Papers, LOC.

"of course the butt" TJ to Richard M. Johnson, March 10, 1808, Thomas Jefferson Papers, LOC.

"Never will it be" *JHT*, V, 666.

"extremely beautiful" Smith, *First Forty Years*, 58.

"Remember the promise" Ibid., 59.

"I am full of plans" TJ to Charles Thomson, December 25, 1808, Charles Thomson Papers, LOC.

"As to Aunt Marks" Martha Jefferson Randolph to TJ, March 2, 1809, Coolidge Collection of Thomas Jefferson Manuscripts, Massachusetts Historical Society.

"a long forgotten Arabian prince" James A. Bear Jr., "The Last Few Days in the Life of Thomas Jefferson," *Magazine of Albemarle County History* 32 (1974), 68.

"memorials of those worthies" TJ to James Bowdoin, April 27, 1805, Thomas Jefferson Papers, LOC.

"cheerfulness and affection" Randall, III, 349.

"to utter a harsh word" Ibid.

"When it grew too dark to read" Ibid., 350.

"We would not speak" Ibid.

"a bundle in his hand" Ibid.

"Our grandfather seemed to read" *TDLTJ*, 345.

"The sun never sees him" *PTJRS*, I, 392–93.

"There is a tranquility about him" Ibid., 395.

"Though I am convinced" Ibid., 263.

"What would become of mankind" Ibid., III, 58.

"I am now on horseback" Ibid., 315.

"luxury of being" Ibid., I, 475.

"I have often thought" Ibid., 205.

"He was not in the habit" Lewis and Onuf, eds., *Sally Hemings and Thomas Jefferson*, 24.

"It is far from uncommon" Elise Lemire, *"Miscegenation": Making Race in America* (Philadelphia, 2002), 11.

CHAPTER TWENTY-THREE

"Every hope" *PTJRS*, IV, 472.

"Tottering over the grave" Ibid., III, 278.

"The friendship of two" Ibid.

"to beat down" Ibid., 305.

"Upon repeating" Ibid., IV, 314. The ensuing scene is drawn from this source.

"A letter from you" Ibid., 428–29.

"So many subjects crowd upon me" Ibid., VI, 277.

"You and I ought not to die before" Ibid., 297.

"With the commonplace topic" Ibid., V, 670.

"In the measures of" Ibid., 3.

"We acted in perfect harmony" Ibid., VI, 566–67.

"On the subject of the history" Cappon, *Adams-Jefferson Letters*, 452.

"We are to have war" *PTJRS*, IV, 472.

"Your message had all" Ibid., 376–77.

"'Wormley, how often'" Randall, III, 332.

"mingling sincerely" Ibid., 446.

"I think, with you" Cappon, *Adams-Jefferson Letters*, 467.

"I dare not look beyond" *PTJRS*, VII, 217–18.

"Some men" TJ to H. Tompkinson (Samuel Kercheval), July 12, 1816. Extract published at Papers of Thomas Jefferson: Retirement Series Digital Archive, www.monticello.org /familyletters (accessed 2011).

"The fact is" TJ to Benjamin Waterhouse, March 3, 1818. Extract published at Papers of Thomas Jefferson: Retirement Series Digital Archive, www.monticello.org /familyletters (accessed 2011).

"When I contemplate" Ibid.

"beyond all price" *JHT*, VI, 177.

"such books as may be" History of the Library, loc.gov/about /history-of-the-library, LOC.

"If we think them not" TJ to William C. Jarvis, September 28, 1820. Extract published at Papers of Thomas Jefferson: Retirement Series Digital Archive, www.monticello.org /familyletters (accessed 2011).

CHAPTER TWENTY-FOUR

"From the Battle of Bunker's Hill" Randall, III, 454.

"The Missouri question" Cappon, *Adams-Jefferson Letters*, 548–49.

"would not cost me" Randall, III, 456.

"Nothing is more certainly written" Jefferson, 44.

"As it is" Randall, III, 456.

"a hideous blot" TJ to William Short, September 8, 1823. Extract published at Papers of Thomas Jefferson: Retirement Series Digital Archive, www.monticello.org /familyletters (accessed 2011).

"There is nothing I would not sacrifice" *PTJRS*, VII, 652.

"I leave its accomplishment" TJ to Frances Wright, August 7, 1825. Extract published at Papers of Thomas Jefferson: Retirement Series Digital Archive, www.monticello.org /familyletters (accessed 2011).

"'My dear Jefferson'" *TJF*, www.monticello.org/site/research -and-collections/lafayettes-visit-to -monticello-1824 (accessed 2012).

"His deeds in the war" Randall, III, 504.

"Born and bred among your fathers" Ibid.

"Adore God" Randall, III, 524–25.

"All eyes are opened" Jefferson, 1517.

"Take care of me when dead" Ibid., 1515.

CHAPTER TWENTY-FIVE
"The loss of Mr. Jefferson" Randall, III, 551.

"the attack would prove" Bear, "Last Few Days in the Life of Thomas Jefferson," 65.

"His mind was always clear" Randall, III, 543.

"George does not" Ibid., 544.

"Lord, now lettest thou thy servant" Ibid., 547.

"Then farewell, my dear" TDLTJ, 429.

"Ah! Doctor" Randall, III, 548.

"No, Doctor, nothing more" Bear, 74.

"This is the Fourth?" Ibid., 75.

"Warn the Committee" Randall, III, 546.

"To me he has been more" Ibid., 551.

"He lives and will live" Ibid., 550.

"Harriet married a white man" TJF, www.monticello.org/site/plantation -and-slavery/harriet-hemings (accessed 2012).

"Thomas Jefferson survives" McCullough, John Adams, 646. The manuscript source is Susan Boylston Adams Clark to Abigail Louisa Smith Adams Johnson, July 9, 1826, A. B. Johnson Papers, Massachusetts Historical Society.

EPILOGUE
"Jefferson's principles" Woodrow Wilson, College and State Educational Literary and Political Papers (1875–1913), II, ed. Ray Stannard Baker and William E. Dodd (New York, 1925), 428.

"If Jefferson was wrong" Parton, Life, iii.

"And I have observed" TJ to William Ludlow, September 6, 1824. Extract published at Papers of Thomas Jefferson: Retirement Series Digital Archive, www.monticello.org/ familyletters (accessed 2012).

JEFFERSON'S WRITINGS
Meacham, Jon. Thomas Jefferson: The Art of Power. New York: Random House, 2012.

A Recipe for Macaroni TJF, monticello.org/site/research-and -collections/macaroni (accessed 2013).

Garden Book, 1766–1824 Jefferson (3). Coolidge Collection of Thomas Jefferson Manuscripts, Massachusetts Historical Society, masshist.org /thomasjeffersonpapers/garden (accessed 2014).

A Letter to a Granddaughter TJF, monticello.org/site/research-and -collections/letter-granddaughters -silkworms (accessed 2014).

Jefferson's Bible web.archive.org /web/20110110200623/

http://etext.lib.virginia.edu
/etcbin/toccer-new2?id=JefJesu
.sgm&images=images
/modeng&data=/texts/english
/modeng/parsed&tag=public&part=
1&division=div1

Paraphrase of Psalm 15 Meacham
(486–487).

*A Summary View of the Rights of
British America* Meacham (74).

Rules of procedure for Congress
Meacham (111).

Notes on the State of Virginia
etext.lib.virginia.edu/etcbin
/toccer-new2?id=JefBv021
.sgm&images=images
/modeng&data=/texts/english
/modeng/parsed&tag=public&part=
1&division=div1

**Jefferson's Autobiography 1743–
1790** web.archive.org
/web/20110221145052/

http://etext.lib.virginia.edu
/etcbin/toccer-new2?id=JefAuto
.xml&images=images
/modeng&data=/texts/english
/modeng/parsed&tag=public&part=
1&division=div1

**"A Decalogue of Canons for
Observation in Practical Life"**
Meacham (487).

Scans of Jefferson's Bible
americanhistory.si.edu/JeffersonBible
/the-book/?page=5&view=scan#dl

PLACES IN THE UNITED STATES

**Jefferson National Expansion
Memorial** (Gateway Arch and park)
www.nps.gov/jeff/index.htm

57 Maiden Lane www.monticello
.org/site/research-and-collections
/new-york-city

West Point www.monticello.org
/site/research-and-collections/united
-states-military-academy-west-point

www.usma.edu/wphistory/SitePages
/Home.aspx

**Lewis and Clark National
Historical Park and Fort Clatsop**
www.pbs.org/lewisandclark/living
/idx_1.html

www.monticello.org/site/jefferson
/lewis-and-clark-expedition

www.nps.gov/lewi/index.htm

www.nps.gov/lewi/planyourvisit
/fortclatsop.htm

www.historylink.org/index
.cfm?DisplayPage=output.cfm&file
_id=9814

American Philosophical Society
www.monticello.org/site/research
-and-collections/american
-philosophical-society

Congress Hall www.nps.gov/inde
/congress-hall.htm

Mount Rushmore www.nps.gov
/moru/historyculture/index.htm

Poplar Forest www.poplarforest
.org/jefferson

University of Virginia Meacham
(469).

Jefferson Memorial washington.org
/DC-guide-to/jefferson-memorial

Library of Congress Meacham
(468); www.loc.gov/visit/maps-and
-floor-plans

PLACES IN FRANCE

Plaque at Hôtel de Langeac
www.monticello.org/site/research
-and-collections/paris-residences

**Thomas Jefferson statue on the
Left Bank** www.panoramio.com
/photo/90165829

BIBLIOGRAPHY

MANUSCRIPT COLLECTIONS

Broadside Collection, Library of Congress, Washington, D.C.

Coolidge Collection of Thomas Jefferson Manuscripts, Massachusetts Historical Society, Boston

Correspondance politique/Affaires politiques jusqu'en 1896: des États-Unis, Archives des affaires étrangères, La Courneuve, France

Andre De Coppet Collection, Princeton University, Princeton, N.J.

Edgehill-Randolph Papers, Special Collections, University of Virginia Library, University of Virginia, Charlottesville, Va.

Augustus Foster Papers, Library of Congress, Washington, D.C.

John Work Garrett Library, Johns Hopkins University, Baltimore

Gratz Collection, Historical Society of Pennsylvania, Philadelphia

The Huntington Library, San Marino, Calif.

Thomas Jefferson Papers, Library of Congress, Washington, D.C.

Papers of Thomas Jefferson, Editorial Files, Princeton University, Princeton, N.J.

Papers of Thomas Jefferson: Retirement Series, Thomas Jefferson Foundation, monticello.org/site/research-and-collections/papers (accessed March 25, 2012)

Papers of Thomas Jefferson: Retirement Series Digital Archive, Thomas Jefferson Foundation, monticello.org/familyletters (accessed March 25, 2012)

Literary and historical manuscripts, Pierpont Morgan Library, New York, N.Y.

National Archives of the United Kingdom, FO 5/14 and 32–58, 353/30 and 60, Kew, Richmond, Surrey, London

Timothy Pickering Papers, Massachusetts Historical Society, Boston

Charles Thomson Papers, Library of Congress, Washington, D.C.

Washburn Collection, Massachusetts Historical Society, Boston

BOOKS CONSULTED

Adams, Henry. *History of the United States of America During the Administrations of Thomas Jefferson.* Edited by Earl N. Harbert. The Library of America, no. 31. New York: Literary Classics of the United States, 1986.

Adams, John. *The Works of John Adams, Second President of the United States: With a Life of the Author, Notes, and Illustrations, by His Grandson Charles Francis Adams.* 10 vols. Boston: Little, Brown, 1850–56.

Adams, William Howard. *The Paris Years of Thomas Jefferson.* New Haven, Conn.: Yale University Press, 2000.

Bear, James A., Jr., ed. *Jefferson at Monticello*. Charlottesville: University of Virginia Press, 1967.

Bowers, Claude G. *Jefferson in Power: The Death Struggle of the Federalists*. Boston: Houghton Mifflin, 1936.

Boyd, Julian P. *Number 7: Alexander Hamilton's Secret Attempts to Control American Foreign Policy, with Supporting Documents*. Princeton, N.J.: Princeton University Press, 1964.

Brodie, Fawn M. *Thomas Jefferson: An Intimate History*. New York: W. W. Norton, 1998.

Brown, Imogene E. *American Aristides: A Biography of George Wythe*. Rutherford, N.J.: Fairleigh Dickinson University Press, 1981.

Brymner, Douglas. *Report on Canadian Archives, 1890*. Ottawa: Brown Chamberlin, 1891.

Bullock, Helen Duprey. *My Head and My Heart: A Little History of Thomas Jefferson and Maria Cosway*. New York: G. P. Putnam's Sons, 1945.

Butterfield, L. H., Wendell D. Garrett, and Marjorie E. Sprague, eds. *Adams Family Correspondence*. 10 vols. to date. The Adams Papers. 2d ser. Cambridge, Mass.: Belknap Press of Harvard University Press, 1963–.

Cappon, Lester J., ed. *The Adams-Jefferson Letters: The Complete Correspondence Between Thomas Jefferson and Abigail and John Adams*. Chapel Hill: Published for the Omohundro Institute of Early American History and Culture, Williamsburg, Va., by the University of North Carolina Press, 1987. First published in 1959 by the University of North Carolina Press.

Cunningham, Noble E. *The Jeffersonian Republicans in Power: Party Operations, 1801–1809*. Chapel Hill: Published for the Omohundro Institute of Early American History and Culture, Williamsburg, Va., by the University of North Carolina Press, 1963.

Dunn, Susan. *Jefferson's Second Revolution: The Election Crisis of 1800 and the Triumph of Republicanism*. Boston: Houghton Mifflin, 2004.

Ellis, Joseph J. *American Creation: Triumphs and Tragedies at the Founding of the Republic*. New York: Alfred A. Knopf, 2007.

Ferling, John. *Adams vs. Jefferson: The Tumultuous Election of 1800*. Pivotal Moments in American History. New York: Oxford University Press, 2004.

———. *Almost a Miracle: The American Victory in the War of Independence*. New York: Oxford University Press, 2009.

Gordon-Reed, Annette. *The Hemingses of Monticello: An American Family*. New York: W. W. Norton, 2008.

Hayes, Kevin J. *The Road to Monticello: The Life and Mind of Thomas Jefferson*. New York: Oxford University Press, 2008.

Hogeland, William. *Declaration: The Nine Tumultuous Weeks When America Became Independent, May 1–July 4, 1776*. New York: Simon and Schuster, 2010.

Jefferson, Thomas. *Jefferson's Memorandum Books: Accounts, with Legal Records and Miscellany, 1767–1826*. Edited by James A. Bear, Jr., and Lucia C. Stanton. 2 vols. The Papers of Thomas Jefferson. 2d ser. Princeton, N.J.: Princeton University Press, 1997.

———. *The Papers of Thomas Jefferson*. Edited by Julian P. Boyd and others. 38 vols. to date. Princeton, N.J.: Princeton University Press, 1950–.

———. *The Papers of Thomas Jefferson. Retirement Series*. Edited by J. Jefferson Looney and others. 8 vols. to date. Princeton, N.J.: Princeton University Press, 2004–.

———. *Thomas Jefferson's Farm Book: With Commentary and Relevant Extracts from Other Writings*. Edited by Edwin Morris Betts. Charlottesville: University of Virginia Press, 1976. First published in 1953 by Princeton University Press.

———. *Thomas Jefferson's Garden Book, 1766–1824: With Relevant Extracts from His Other Writings*. Edited by Edwin Morris Betts. Philadelphia: American Philosophical Society, 1944.

———. *The Words of Thomas Jefferson*. Charlottesville, Va.: Thomas Jefferson Foundation, 2008.

———. *Writings*. Edited by Merrill D. Peterson. The Library of America, no. 17. New York: Literary Classics of the United States, 1984.

Kaminski, John P., ed. *The Founders on the Founders: Word Portraits from the American Revolutionary Era*. Charlottesville: University of Virginia Press, 2008.

King, Rufus. *The Life and Correspondence of Rufus King: Comprising His Letters, Private and Official, His Public Documents, and His Speeches*. 6 vols. Edited by Charles R. King. New York: Da Capo Press, 1971. First published in 1894–1900 by G. P. Putnam's Sons.

Kranish, Michael. *Flight from Monticello: Thomas Jefferson at War*. New York: Oxford University Press, 2010.

Lemire, Elise. *"Miscegenation": Making Race in America*. Philadelphia: University of Pennsylvania Press, 2002.

Lewis, Jan Ellen, and Peter S. Onuf, eds. *Sally Hemings and Thomas Jefferson: History, Memory, and Civic Culture*. Jeffersonian America. Charlottesville: University of Virginia Press, 1999.

Lewis, Meriwether, and William Clark. *The Journals of Lewis and Clark*. Edited by John Bakeless. New York: Penguin Group, 1964.

Malone, Dumas. *Jefferson and His Time*. 6 vols. Boston: Little, Brown, 1948–81. Vol. I, *Jefferson the Virginian*, 1948. Vol. 2, *Jefferson and the Rights of Man*, 1951. Vol. 3, *Jefferson and the Ordeal of Liberty*, 1962. Vol. 4, *Jefferson the President: First Term, 1801–1805*, 1970. Vol. 5, *Jefferson the President: Second Term, 1805–1809*, 1974. Vol. 6, *The Sage of Monticello*, 1981.

Marshall, John. *The Papers of John Marshall*. Edited by Herbert A. Johnson and others. 12 vols. to date. Chapel Hill: University of North Carolina Press, 1974–.

Mayer, Henry. *A Son of Thunder: Patrick Henry and the American Republic.* New York: Grove Press, 2001. First published in 1986 by Franklin Watts.

McCullough, David. *John Adams.* New York: Simon and Schuster, 2001.

McDonnell, Michael A. *The Politics of War: Race, Class, and Conflict in Revolutionary Virginia.* Chapel Hill: Published for the Omohundro Institute of Early American History and Culture, Williamsburg, Va., by the University of North Carolina Press, 2007.

Middlekauff, Robert. *The Glorious Cause: The American Revolution, 1763–1789.* Revised and expanded ed. The Oxford History of the United States. New York: Oxford University Press, 2005.

Moore, Roy, and Alma Moore. *Thomas Jefferson's Journey to the South of France.* New York: Stewart, Tabori and Chang, 1999.

Morgan, Edmund S. *Virginians at Home: Family Life in the Eighteenth Century.* Williamsburg in America Series, no. 2. Charlottesville, Va.: Dominion Books, 1963. First published in 1952 by Colonial Williamsburg, Williamsburg, Va.

Morgan, Edmund S., and Helen M. Morgan. *The Stamp Act Crisis: Prologue to Revolution.* With a new preface by Edmund S. Morgan. Chapel Hill: Published for the Omohundro Institute of Early American History and Culture, Williamsburg, Va., by the University of North Carolina Press, 1995. First published in 1953 by the University of North Carolina Press.

Peterson, Merrill D., ed. *Visitors to Monticello.* Charlottesville: University of Virginia Press, 1989.

Randall, Henry S. *The Life of Thomas Jefferson.* 3 vols. The American Scene. New York: De Capo Press, 1972. First published in 1858 by Derby and Jackson.

Randolph, Sarah N. *The Domestic Life of Thomas Jefferson.* New York: Harper and Brothers, 1871.

Reardon, John J. *Peyton Randolph, 1721–1775: One Who Presided.* Durham, N.C.: Carolina Academic Press, 1982.

Scharff, Virginia. *The Women Jefferson Loved.* New York: Harper, 2010.

Seale, William. *The President's House: A History.* Vol. 1. Washington, D.C.: White House Historical Association with the cooperation of the National Geographic Society, 1986.

Smith, James Morton. *Freedom's Fetters: The Alien and Sedition Laws and American Civil Liberties.* Ithaca, N.Y.: Cornell University Press, 1966.

Smith, Margaret Bayard. *The First Forty Years of Washington Society in the Family Letters of Margaret Bayard Smith.* Edited by Gaillard Hunt. American Classics. New York: Frederick Ungar, 1965. First published in 1906 by Charles Scribner's Sons.

Sofaer, Abraham D. *War, Foreign Affairs, and Constitutional Power: The Origins.* Cambridge, Mass.: Ballinger, 1976.

Stein, Susan R. *The Worlds of Thomas Jefferson at Monticello.* New York: H. N. Abrams, in association with the Thomas Jefferson Memorial Foundation, 1993.

Troy, Gil, Arthur M. Schlesinger, Jr., and Fred L. Israel, eds. *History of American Presidential Elections, 1789–2008.* 4th ed. Vol. I, *1789–1868.* New York: Facts on File, 2010.

Unger, Harlow Giles. *John Hancock: Merchant King and American Patriot.* New York: John Wiley and Sons, 2000.

Webster, Daniel. *The Writings and Speeches of Daniel Webster.* Edited by Fletcher Webster. 18 vols. Boston: Little, Brown, 1903.

Wood, Gordon S. *Empire of Liberty: A History of the Early Republic, 1789–1815.* The Oxford History of the United States. New York: Oxford University Press, 2009.

ARTICLES, ESSAYS, REVIEWS, AND WEBSITES

Bear, James A., Jr. "The Last Few Days in the Life of Thomas Jefferson." *Magazine of Albemarle County History* 32 (1974): 63–79.

Dabney, Virginius. "Jouett Outrides Tarleton, and Saves Jefferson from Capture." *Scribner's Magazine,* June 1928, 690–98.

"Dinner Etiquette." Thomas Jefferson Encyclopedia, Thomas Jefferson Foundation. monticello.org/site /research-and-collections/dinner -etiquette (accessed April 7, 2012).

"Fishing." Thomas Jefferson Encyclopedia, Thomas Jefferson Foundation. monticello.org/site /research-and-collections/fishing (accessed April 2, 2012).

"Journal of a French Traveller in the Colonies, 1765." Parts 1 and 2. *The American Historical Review* 26 (July 1921): 726–47; 27 (October 1921): 70–89.

"Lafayette's Visit to Monticello (1824)." Thomas Jefferson Encyclopedia, Thomas Jefferson Foundation. monticello.org/site /research-and-collections /lafayettes-visit-to-monticello -1824 (accessed April 8, 2012).

"Martha Wayles Skelton Jefferson." Thomas Jefferson Encyclopedia, Thomas Jefferson Foundation. monticello.org/site/jefferson /martha-wayles-skelton-jefferson (accessed 2012).

"Plantation and Slavery." Thomas Jefferson Foundation. monticello .org/site/plantation-and-slavery (accessed April 2, 2012).

Report of the Committee, Appointed to Inquire Into the Conduct of Brigadier Gen. J. Wilkinson: May 1st, 1810. Washington City: Printed by R. C. Weightman, 1810.

ILLUSTRATION CREDITS

PROLOGUE

Feather © Kerem Yucel via FreeImages.com

Declaration of Independence, by John Trumbull, 1818, Rotunda of the U.S. Capitol/Architect of the Capitol

Thomas Jefferson, 1791, by Charles Willson Peale, The Granger Collection, NYC, courtesy of Independence National Historical Park

Ivory note cards © Thomas Jefferson Foundation at Monticello, photograph by Edward Owen

Jefferson Sketch of the First House, or Monticello I © Thomas Jefferson Foundation at Monticello

CHAPTER ONE

Map of Virginia and Maryland, drawn by Joshua Fry and Peter Jefferson, printed by Sayer and Jefferys, c. 1776 © Thomas Jefferson Foundation at Monticello, photograph by Edward Owen

Ramsden theodolite © Thomas Jefferson Foundation at Monticello

Illustration from *Voyage Round the World in the Years MDCCXL, I, II, III, IV.* By George Anson. Compiled by Richard Walter/J. Mason © National Library of France

Shadwell marker © Thomas Jefferson Foundation at Monticello

Monticello archaeological site at Shadwell © Thomas Jefferson Foundation at Monticello

Wren Hall, the College of William and Mary, lithograph by Crump, after a painting by Thomas Millington, c. 1850 © The Colonial Williamsburg Foundation

CHAPTER TWO

Detail of courtyard at the College of William and Mary, modern impression taken from the original 1740s copperplate © The Colonial Williamsburg Foundation

Portrait of William Small, by Tilly Kettle © Muscarelle Museum of Art at the College of William and Mary in Virginia

George Wythe, 1888, by Albert Rosenthal, after William S. Leney, The Granger Collection, NYC

Portrait of Francis Fauquier, lieutenant governor of Virginia in the American colonies, c. 1757, by Richard Wilson © Coram in the care of the Foundling Museum, London/The Bridgeman Art Library

Aerial view of the reconstructed Governor's Palace, Williamsburg, Virginia © The Colonial Williamsburg Foundation

Peyton Randolph, Library of Congress Prints and Photographs Division, Washington, D.C.

Front elevation of the Raleigh Tavern
© The Colonial Williamsburg
Foundation

CHAPTER THREE
Anti–Stamp Act, Boston, 1765,
German engraving by Daniel
Chodowiecki, 1784, The Granger
Collection, NYC

Patrick Henry making his famous
speech in the House of Burgesses,
after Peter Fred Rothermel,
Private Collection/The Stapleton
Collection/The Bridgeman Art
Library

Garden Book, 1766–1824, page 5,
by Thomas Jefferson, Thomas
Jefferson Papers: An Electronic
Archive, Boston, Mass. ©
Massachusetts Historical Society

CHAPTER FOUR
House of Burgesses in the Capitol,
Williamsburg, Virginia, photograph
by Frances Benjamin Johnston,
Library of Congress Prints and
Photographs Division, Washington,
D.C.

"Sandy" ad from *Virginia Gazette,* 1769
© Virginia Historical Society

Gardens at Monticello © Teresa
O'Connor

CHAPTER FIVE
Hand telescope © Thomas Jefferson
Foundation at Monticello,
photograph by H. Andrew Johnson

Monticello kitchen © Thomas
Jefferson Foundation at Monticello,
photograph by Philip Beaurline

Monticello graveyard marker © John
Works

CHAPTER SIX
The Destruction of Tea at Boston Harbor,
1773, copy of lithograph by Sarony
& Major, 1846 © National Archives

"Join, or Die," by Benjamin Franklin,
Pennsylvania Gazette (Philadelphia),
May 9, 1754, Library of Congress,
Washington, D.C.

Title page of *A Summary View of the
Rights of British America,* by Thomas
Jefferson, 1774, Rare Books and
Special Collections Division of the
Library of Congress, Washington,
D.C.

Portrait of George III in his
coronation robes, c. 1760, by Allan
Ramsay, Private Collection/The
Bridgeman Art Library

Portrait of John Murray, 4th Earl
of Dunmore, 1929, by Charles
Xavier Harris (copy of original
by Sir Joshua Reynolds), Virginia
Historical Society, Richmond,
Virginia, USA/The Bridgeman Art
Library

Map of town and harbor of Boston,
1775, Library of Congress
Geography and Map Division,
Washington, D.C.

Congress voting on the Declaration
of Independence, engraving by
Edward Savage, after a painting
by Robert Edge Pine, Library of
Congress Prints and Photographs
Division, Washington, D.C.

CHAPTER SEVEN
Battle of Bunker Hill, 1909, by
E. Percy Moran, Library of Congress
Prints and Photographs Division,
Washington, D.C.

Independence Hall in Philadelphia,
PA © Marco Rubino via
Shutterstock

CHAPTER EIGHT

John Adams, 1788, by Mather Brown
© Boston Athenaeum, USA/The
Bridgeman Art Library

Writing the Declaration of
Independence in 1776, by Jean
Leon Gerome Ferris, Virginia
Historical Society, Richmond,
Virginia, USA/The Bridgeman Art
Library

House of Jacob Graff, Jr., where
Jefferson wrote the Declaration of
Independence in 1776, by Benjamin
Ridgway Evans, courtesy of the
Historical Society of Pennsylvania
Medium Graphics Collection

"Original Rough Draft" of the
Declaration of Independence, June
1776, Thomas Jefferson Papers,
Manuscript Division, Library of
Congress, Washington, D.C.

Benjamin Franklin, attributed to
Jean Valade, after 1778 original
by Joseph-Silfrede Duplessis ©
Thomas Jefferson Foundation at
Monticello

Engraving of the Declaration of
Independence © National Archives

CHAPTER NINE

Portrait of James Madison, by
Gilbert Stuart, 1804, The Colonial
Williamsburg Foundation, Gift of
Mrs. George S. Robbins, 1945–23

Benedict Arnold, copy of engraving
by H. B. Hall after John Trumbull,
published 1879, 1931–1932 ©
National Archives

Isaac Granger Jefferson,
daguerreotype, 1847, accession
#2041, Special Collections,
University of Virginia Library,
Charlottesville, Virginia

CHAPTER TEN

Silver plate by Lamine © Thomas
Jefferson Foundation at Monticello

Siege of Yorktown, October 17, 1781,
1836, by Louis Charles Auguste
Couder, Chateau de Versailles,
France/Giraudon/The Bridgeman
Art Library

Servant bell, late eighteenth century,
Moorland-Spingarn Research
Center, Howard University

CHAPTER ELEVEN

Fossil of mastodon upper mandible
© Thomas Jefferson Foundation at
Monticello, photograph by Edward
Owen

Grille de Chaillot, Paris, with the
Hôtel de Langeac at left © Thomas
Jefferson Foundation at Monticello

Tripolitan War, 1804, from a painting
by Dennis Malone Carter, The
Granger Collection, NYC

CHAPTER TWELVE

Façade of Versailles Palace © Pack-
Shot via Shutterstock

Marquis Marie-Joseph Paul Yves
Roch Gilbert du Motier de
Lafayette, 1790, by Joseph Boze ©
Massachusetts Historical Society,
Boston, MA, USA/The Bridgeman
Art Library

Maria Cosway, engraving by Valentine
Green, after Maria Cosway self-
portrait, 1787, Carol Burnell
Collection

Abigail Adams, 1785, by Mather Brown, The Granger Collection, NYC

CHAPTER THIRTEEN

Scene at the Signing of the Constitution of the United States, by artist Howard Chandler Christy © Architect of the Capitol, Washington, DC

Shays' Rebellion © Getty/Hulton Archive

John Adams, from a painting by Alonzo Chappel, Special Collections Research Center, University of Chicago Library

The Taking of the Bastille, July 14, 1789, French School (eighteenth century), Chateau de Versailles, France/Giraudon/The Bridgeman Art Library

Declaration of the Rights of Man and of the Citizen, Jean-Jacques-Francois Le Barbier © Musée Carnavalet/Roger-Viollet

King Louis XVI of France on his coronation day, June 11, 1775, c. 1787, The Granger Collection, NYC

Portrait of Marie Antoinette, Queen of France, 1775, by Jean-Baptiste Andre Gautier D'Agoty, Chateau de Versailles, France/Giraudon/The Bridgeman Art Library

CHAPTER FOURTEEN

Federal Hall, Wall Street & Trinity Church, New York, in 1789 © The New York Public Library

Thomas Mann Randolph Jr., American School (eighteenth century), Virginia Historical Society, Richmond, Virginia, USA/The Bridgeman Art Library

George Washington, 1784–86, by Joseph Wright and John Trumbull © Massachusetts Historical Society, Boston, MA, USA/The Bridgeman Art Library

Alexander Hamilton, 1806, by John Trumbull, The Granger Collection, NYC

Marie-Antoinette and Her Children, c. 1787, The Granger Collection, NYC

Magna Carta, 1297 © National Archives

Louis XVI being led to the guillotine at the time of his execution, Library of Congress Prints and Photographs Division, Washington, D.C.

Alexander Hamilton, by Giuseppe Ceracchi, 1794 © Thomas Jefferson Foundation at Monticello

Thomas Jefferson, by Jean-Antoine Houdon © Thomas Jefferson Foundation at Monticello

CHAPTER FIFTEEN

Washington with Jefferson and Hamilton, 1872, by Constantino Brumidi, Senate Reception Room of the U.S. Capitol/Architect of the Capitol

Drawing of slave quarters at Monticello, 1770, by Thomas Jefferson, The Granger Collection, NYC

A Moment on Mulberry Row, by Nathaniel K. Gibbs, 1997

Whiskey Rebellion, 1794, oil painting, c. 1795, attributed to Frederick Kemmelmeyer, The Granger Collection, NYC

John Jay, 1794, by Gilbert Stuart, The Granger Collection, NYC

CHAPTER SIXTEEN

Congressional Pugilists, 1798, Library of Congress Prints and Photographs Division, Washington, D.C.

Title page of *The Prospect Before Us*, the anti-Federalist tract by political pamphleteer and journalist James T. Callender, courtesy of the General Collection, Beinecke Rare Book and Manuscript Library, Yale University, New Haven, Connecticut

CHAPTER SEVENTEEN

Death of Washington, lithograph by James Baillie, c. 1845, courtesy of Mount Vernon Ladies Association

Aaron Burr, by John Vanderlyn, early nineteenth century, The Granger Collection, NYC

John Marshall, by Albert Newsam, after Henry Inman, 1831, Emmet Collection, Miriam and Ira D. Wallach Division of Arts, Prints and Photographs, The New York Public Library, Astor, Lenox and Tilden Foundations

Presidential campaign banner, 1800, The Granger Collection, NYC

CHAPTER EIGHTEEN

Thomas Jefferson, President of the United States, engraving by Cornelius Tiebout after a painting by Rembrandt Peale, Library of Congress Prints and Photographs Division, Washington, D.C.

Northern mockingbird © Stubblefield Photography via Shutterstock

Design for the President's House competition, c. 1792, by Thomas Jefferson, The Granger Collection, NYC

A view of the President's House in the City of Washington after the conflagration of August 24, 1814, engraver William Strickland, artist George Munger, Library of Congress Prints and Photographs Division, Washington, D.C.

George Washington, President of the United States, engraving by H. S. Sadd after a painting by G. Stuart, Library of Congress Prints and Photographs Division, Washington, D.C.

Waistcoat © Thomas Jefferson Foundation at Monticello, photograph courtesy of The Colonial Williamsburg Foundation

A Sea Fight with Barbary Corsairs, by Lorenzo a Castro © Dulwich Picture Gallery, London

Portrait of Meriwether Lewis, by Charles Willson Peale, c. 1807–08 © Independence National Historic Park

Portrait of William Clark, by Charles Willson Peale, c. 1807 © Independence National Historic Park

CHAPTER NINETEEN

The Recorder, 1802 © Lehigh University Digital Library and the Library of Virginia

Margaret Bayard Smith, after the portrait by Charles Bird King, in the possession of her grandson, J. Henley Smith, Washington, from *The First Forty Years of Washington Society*, by Gaillard Hunt (ed.)

Napoleon Crossing the Alps, by Jacques-Louis David, Chateau de Versailles, France/Peter Willi/The Bridgeman Art Library

Louisiana Purchase, 1803, *Under My Wings Everything Prospers*, view of the city of New Orleans, celebrating President Jefferson's Louisiana Purchase, oil on canvas, 1803, by Boqueto de Woiseri, The Granger Collection, NYC

James Monroe, 1817, by Gilbert Stuart, The Granger Collection, NYC

Louisiana Purchase map, U.S. 40-4, Old Map File, Record Group 49, Records of the Bureau of Land Management (General Land Office), Cartographic Section, National Archives at College Park, MD

Treaty Between the United States and France for the Cession of Louisiana, April 30, 1803, Treaty Series 86 AO/National Archives and Records Administration, Washington, D.C.

Captain Lewis & Clark holding a council with the Indians, Library of Congress, Washington, D.C.

CHAPTER TWENTY

Duel between Aaron Burr and Alexander Hamilton, David B. Scott, *A School History of the United States* (New York: American Book Company, 1884) 243 © private collection of Ray Winkelman via ETC

Governor George Clinton, 1814, by Ezra Ames © Collection of the New-York Historical Society, USA/The Bridgeman Art Library

"Lewis & Clark at Three Forks," by Edgar Samuel Paxson © Montana Historical Society

Fort Clatsop © Nagel Photography via Shutterstock

Lewis and Clark on the Lower Columbia River, 1905, by Charles Marion Russell, Private Collection/Peter Newark American Pictures/The Bridgeman Art Library

CHAPTER TWENTY-ONE

Aaron Burr, head-and-shoulders portrait, facing left, print created/published c. 1899, Library of Congress Prints and Photographs Division, Washington, D.C.

Engagement between USS *Chesapeake* and HMS *Shannon*, 1 June 1813, aquatint by Jeakes after a painting by Thomas Whitcombe © U.S. Naval Academy Museum

Charles Cotesworth Pinckney, Library of Congress Prints and Photographs Division, Washington, D.C.

CHAPTER TWENTY-TWO

James Madison, President of the United States, engraving by David Edwin after a painting by Thomas Sully, Library of Congress Prints and Photographs Division, Washington, D.C.

Monticello, second version (plan and west elevation), by Robert Mills, 1803, N155, K156/original manuscript from the Coolidge Collection of Thomas Jefferson Manuscripts, Massachusetts Historical Society

Jefferson's bedchamber © Thomas Jefferson Foundation at Monticello, photograph by Carol Highsmith

Christopher Columbus, after a painting in the Uffizi, Florence, 1788, by Calendi, Giuseppe © Massachusetts Historical Society, Boston, MA, USA/The Bridgeman Art Library

Sir Walter Raleigh, 1787, by or after Edward Alcock © Thomas Jefferson Foundation at Monticello, photograph by Edward Owen

Sir Isaac Newton, by Sir Godfrey Kneller, Bt, 1702 © National Portrait Gallery, London/NPG 2881

Monticello hall © Thomas Jefferson Foundation at Monticello, photograph by Robert C. Lautman

Monticello parlor © Thomas Jefferson Foundation at Monticello, photograph by Robert C. Lautman

Farm Book, 1774–1824, page 24, by Thomas Jefferson, Thomas Jefferson Papers: An Electronic Archive, Boston, Mass. © Massachusetts Historical Society

CHAPTER TWENTY-THREE

Benjamin Rush, by Thomas Sully, Smithsonian American Art Museum, Washington, D.C./Art Resource, NY

Portrait of John Adams, after Gilbert Stuart, Musée franco-américaine du Château de Blérancourt, Chauny, France/The Bridgeman Art Library

General Andrew Jackson at the Battle of New Orleans, artist unknown © Stock Montage/SuperStock

Dolley Payne Madison, by Gilbert Stuart, 1804, White House Historical Association (White House Collection)

Jefferson's bifocal eyeglasses with lenses and green-tinted spectacles © Thomas Jefferson Foundation at Monticello, photograph by Edward Owen

Reading Room, Library of Congress © Galina Mikhalishina via Shutterstock

University of Virginia Rotunda and Lawn, engraving by J. Serz, published by C. Bohn, 1856, accession #RG-30/I/8.801, University of Virginia Visual History Collection, Special Collections, University of Virginia Library, Charlottesville, Virginia

CHAPTER TWENTY-FOUR

Archaeology at Monticello on Mulberry Row © Thomas Jefferson Foundation at Monticello

Slave and Free Areas After the Missouri Compromise, Jacques W. Redway, FRGS, *The Redway School History*, downloaded from Maps ETC

Portrait of Marquis de Lafayette (1779–80), by Charles Willson Peale © Independence National Historic Park, Portrait Collection

Signatures on the Declaration of Independence © National Archives

CHAPTER TWENTY-FIVE

Thomas Jefferson Randolph, c. 1808, by Charles Willson Peale © Thomas Jefferson Foundation at Monticello, photograph by Edward Owen

Martha Jefferson Randolph, 1823, by James Westhall Ford © Thomas Jefferson Foundation at Monticello, photograph by Edward Owen

Epitaph by Thomas Jefferson, c. March 1826, Thomas Jefferson Papers, Manuscript Division, Library of Congress, Washington, D.C.

Announcement of sale of Jefferson's estate, courtesy American Antiquarian Society

EPILOGUE
Jefferson Memorial in Washington, D.C. © Orhan Cam via Shutterstock

IN JEFFERSON'S WORLD
Johann Sebastian Bach © Nicku via Shutterstock

Spinning jenny © Dario Sabljak via Shutterstock

James Watt © Georgios Kollidas via Shutterstock

Monument of Adam Smith © Heartland Arts via Shutterstock

Montgolfier brothers' hot-air balloon from 1783, picture from Meyers Lexicon Books © Nicku via Shutterstock

Mary Wollstonecraft, detail of an oil painting on canvas by John Opie, c. 1797 © National Portrait Gallery, London

Napoleon Bonaparte, engraving from *Harper's Monthly* magazine © Stocksnapper via Shutterstock

Statue of George Washington in Boston Public Garden © Jorge Salcedo via Shutterstock

Liberty Bell © Edwin Verrin via Shutterstock

Betsy Ross House © Olivier Le Queinec via Shutterstock

Charleville musket, surcharged *U.S.* © Armed Forces History, National Museum of American History, Smithsonian Institution

Canteen © The Second Pennsylvania Regiment and The Forty-Third Regiment of Foot, Inc.

Soldiers in Uniform, by Jean Baptiste Antoine de Verger © Anne S. K. Brown Military Collection, Brown University Library

George Washington's dentures © New York Academy of Medicine via Mount Vernon

Molly Pitcher, originally published by Currier & Ives © Library of Congress Prints and Photographs Division, Washington, D.C.

Thomas Jefferson ("maccaroni") machine with instructions for making pasta) holograph drawing and text, 1787 © Thomas Jefferson Foundation at Monticello

Revolving book stand © Thomas Jefferson Foundation at Monticello

Lap desk © Smithsonian Institution

Sundial © Thomas Jefferson Foundation at Monticello

Wheel cipher © Thomas Jefferson Foundation at Monticello, made by Ronald Kirby

INDEX

Jon Meacham is the author of the number one *New York Times* bestseller *Thomas Jefferson: The Art of Power*. He received the Pulitzer Prize for *American Lion,* his bestselling biography of Andrew Jackson. He is also the author of the *New York Times* bestsellers *Franklin and Winston* and *American Gospel*. Meacham is an executive editor and executive vice president of Random House and a contributing editor of *Time*. Born in Chattanooga, he was educated at the University of the South and lives with his wife and three children in Nashville and Sewanee.